THE MILLIONAIRE MONEY SECRET

47 WAYS TO INVEST LIKE THE TOP 1%

DAVID FRAZIER

REAL DAILY

TABLE OF CONTENTS

Basics You Need to Know 9

Investing Before the Age of 40 26

The Middle Years of Work,
Investing and Retirement Planning 38

Investing for Retirement in Your 50s..52

The Homestretch—Investing for
Retirement in Your 60s and Beyond...63

Opportunities and Threats for Your Retirement 72

Live On More During Retirement 84

Appendix A. Real Estate Property Taxes by State 91

Appendix B. Sales Taxes by State..93

Everybody hates paying taxes. It doesn't matter if you are 19 and just started your first job or if you are 79 and retired. Nobody enjoys paying taxes, but they are inevitable.

Can you imagine being retired and getting hit with a huge tax bill? Unfortunately, it happens to more and more retirees each and every year. You pay taxes on Social Security income if it exceeds certain thresholds. You have to pay taxes on your pension income and any distributions from your IRA and 401(k). And, depending upon where you live, you could be paying federal, state and local taxes on all those different sources of income.

Despite your best efforts, you are more than likely going to have to pay some form of taxes every year of your life. However, there are ways to minimize how much you have to pay, especially during your retirement years.

The objective of this book is to help you build and grow a portfolio that will get you to retirement and through

retirement. It will show you how to invest at various points in your life, the adjustments you will want to make as your get closer to retirement and changes to make in retirement to minimize your taxes.

In order for this goal to be achieved, there are some basic concepts about investing that you will need to know. Things like knowing the difference between stocks and bonds, and the differences between common stock and preferred stock. You will also want to understand the different asset allocation philosophies and how they can help you manage your money, and how and when to be more aggressive.

Over the next chapters, we will guide you through this process. The first part of the book is about growing and protecting your portfolio, and understanding investment concepts. The second part of the book will show you how to maximize your income and minimize your taxes during your retirement years.

Let's get started.

CHAPTER 1.
BASICS YOU NEED TO KNOW

Depending upon your job and your field of study, you might not have taken any finance classes in college. If you were a business major, you were at least exposed to the basics of all the different fields—finance, economics, management, and so on. If you were an engineering, science or liberal arts major, you might not have taken a single class in any of these fields of study, just like an economics major wouldn't have taken a basic engineering class.

With this in mind, let's go over some of the basics of investing.

One of the most important lessons of investing is knowing the difference between stock investments and bond investments. Sometimes you will hear stocks called equity investments and bond investments as fixed-income. Stocks are called equity investments

---

REAL DAILY

because you are buying equity in a company when you buy shares of stock. You are a part owner of the company.

When you buy bonds of a company, you are a creditor to the company. You will receive regular interest payments from them and you receive your principal back at the maturity date. The value of the bonds can fluctuate from the time they are issued until they mature, but the value at maturity will be a set amount.

One of the biggest differences between stock ownership and bond ownership is what happens in the case of bankruptcy. If for some reason the company you invested in gets in trouble and is forced to liquidate, the bond holders get paid before the stock holders get anything. This makes debt instruments considerably safer than equity investments. You also can buy the bonds from the federal government and state and local governments, as well as foreign governments. Any time you buy a bond, though, you become a lender to the entity that issued the bond. Of course, there are numerous other forms of investment vehicles, but most of them come back to whether they are stock or bond investments. You can invest in mutual funds, exchange-traded funds (ETF), and other pooled investments, but they likely are invested in either the stocks of companies or the bonds of companies or governments.

Regardless of whether you are investing in stocks, bonds, ETFs, or mutual funds, your profits on your investments will come in three forms: capital gains, dividends and interest. You get a capital gain when you sell a stock or bond for more than you originally paid for it. Dividends are excess profits pay out to stockholders. Interest is paid to holders of bonds and other debt instruments.

TAX IMPACT

The different forms of profit from investments are taxed very differently. Capital gains are taxed based on how long you held the investment. For investments held for 365 days or less, the gains are taxed at your regular tax bracket. If held for 366 days or more, the tax rate is 0%, 15% or 20%, depending upon the income tax bracket you fall in. Interest from bonds is considered interest income and is taxed at your normal income tax rate. However, if the interest comes from municipal bonds, the interest can be free from federal, state and local taxes. Dividends take two forms: qualified and non-qualified. Qualified dividends are taxed the same as a long-term capital gain and thus "qualify" for the lower tax bracket. Non-qualified dividends, as the name implies, don't qualify for this special treatment. There will be more on these topics throughout the book.

THE RISK/REWARD RELATIONSHIP AND HOW IT CHANGES

The general rule for investments is the higher the risk an investment involves, the higher the potential return of that investment. The relationship between risk and reward is an important one and each investor's tolerance for risk will vary. Some investors are very conservative and have very little risk tolerance.

Others are more risk-tolerant and are willing to be more aggressive with their investments. As you age, too, your personal tolerance for risk tends to change. When you get closer to retirement age, there is less time to make up any losses you may incur. As a result, investors usually become more conservative as time passes. They become risk-averse.

All investments come with some level of risk. And each investment category has different risk levels within them. As discussed above, corporate bonds are riskier than federal government bonds, known as Treasury bonds. The same is true within the world of stocks. Large-cap stocks, the stocks of big, well-established companies, are generally less risky than small-cap stocks, the stocks of small firms. Large-cap U.S. stocks are less risky than large-cap stocks from an emerging market country. Utility stocks, such as electricity companies, are less risky than small, start-up biotech stocks, and so on.

The same holds true for bonds. When investing in the bonds of different companies or countries, there is a big difference in the risk levels of these investments. The U.S. government issues a lot of debt,

but investing in the bonds of the federal government is considered to be one of the safest investments you can make. Just ask yourself, "Do I have more confidence in the U.S. government paying me back, or the government of Argentina paying me back?" For most investors, the answer is simple: Uncle Sam is good for it.

The same principles apply to buying bonds in state and local governments. Certain states are considered safer investments than others and some cities are considered safer than others. These same types of risks apply to corporate bonds. Creditors have far more faith in Apple or Goldman Sachs paying them back for a loan than they do a tiny startup with no profits to show.

Because of these various risk levels for bonds, there are bond rating agencies that assign different grades to all bonds that are issued. The two main rating agencies are Moody's and Standard & Poor's (S&P). They control approximately 80% of the market in the ratings business.

Both Moody's and S&P have 21 letter grades they can assign bonds, but these basically break down in to two categories: investment grade and non-investment grade. The highest rating from Moody's is "Aaa"

and the highest from S&P is "AAA." The lowest grade by each agency is a "C." There are 19 other sub-ratings, ranging between the best and the worst.

Generally, the higher a bond is rated, the less interest the issuer has to pay to attract investors. So a bond with a "AAA" rating from S&P or a "Aaa" rating from Moody's will pay a lower interest rate than one with a "C" rating from either one. This is another basic tenant of investing: The more risk involved, the greater the possible return. Since a lower-rated bond implies more risk, the borrower must pay the investor more to use their money.

One of the easiest ways to mitigate risk is through diversification. By building a portfolio of numerous stocks, you lessen the risk of losing everything should any one of those companies go under. If you are invested in just one stock and that company goes in to bankruptcy, you could lose the entire investment. If your money is invested in 10 companies, however, it is highly unlikely that all 10 will go out of business. The same philosophy can be applied to bonds and all other asset classes.

Mutual funds and exchange-traded funds were mentioned earlier. These represent one of the easiest ways to diversify your portfolio with one investment. When you invest in a fund, you are buying the shares of the fund. The fund, in turn, invests the money into a portfolio of stocks or bonds and possibly both. Mutual funds used to be the preferred style of pooling investments, but ETFs have gained considerable ground in the last decade. Asset flows into ETFs have been exceeding mutual fund inflows for several years now.

The reason for the growth in ETFs is no big surprise either. Most ETFs have lower management fees than mutual funds and you can trade ETFs on an intra-day basis. With mutual funds you have to wait until the end of the day to buy or sell them. And with the number of ETFs that have been created in the last 20 years, there are funds that represent almost every sector and every market in the world. There are also ETFs that hold different bond classes, bonds from different countries, different states and municipal bonds.

CAUTION: Not all ETFs are low-cost, and some can be tremendously high-risk. The ETF structure has been adopted to create some fairly speculative investments that use leverage to seek very high short-term gains, thus also the potential for very high losses. So, while most ETFs are a good choice for the retirement investor, the label "ETF" does not automatically mean "better" or "safer" for most people. Be sure to research any recommendations you get before investing. Buying one ETF or mutual fund gives you instant diversification in one asset class, but you can also use them to build a portfolio of different funds. You can build a portfolio of 10 ETFs that represent the 10 main economic sectors. This would give you small stakes in hundreds, if not thousands, of companies. You won't be a direct shareholder in the companies with voting rights, but the fund will benefit if the stocks rise in value.

While ETFs have gained in popularity, mutual funds are still the main investment vehicles within company-sponsored retirement plans. That is why it is necessary to talk about both of them. Regardless if you use ETFs or mutual funds, the general idea and purpose of the funds is to provide diversification for the buyers of the funds.

TAX IMPACT

ETFs tend to be more tax efficient than comparable mutual funds, especially in a non-retirement investment account. Even though they are considered the same by the Internal Revenue Service, ETFs have an advantage because there are fewer taxable events. The reason for this is because of the way they are structured. A mutual fund manager has to re-balance the portfolio constantly to accommodate inflows and outflows from investors. When an investment is sold for a gain within the fund, it creates a capital gain. ETF managers don't face this same problem as they accommodate investor inflows and outflows by creating more "creation units" or redeeming them. Creation units are simply baskets of assets that closely replicate the entire portfolio. This results in the ETF investor experiencing fewer capital gains if a security is sold within the fund.

REAL DAILY

THE IMPORTANCE OF ASSET ALLOCATION

Asset allocation is a very important part of your investing life cycle. It may sound like a daunting term, "asset allocation," but it is really just a way of saying how you divide your investments up in to different categories: How much you put into stocks versus how much you put into bonds. How much do you put into growth stocks versus how much you put into large-cap stocks. The term sounds much more intimidating than what happens in practice.

When it comes to deciding on your asset allocation, there are a number of variables that you have to consider. First, there are different theories with similar ideas about asset allocation. There is strategic asset allocation, for instance, and there is tactical asset allocation. Strategic allocation focuses more on the investor and their age. Tactical asset allocation is more concerned about the market and the timing of

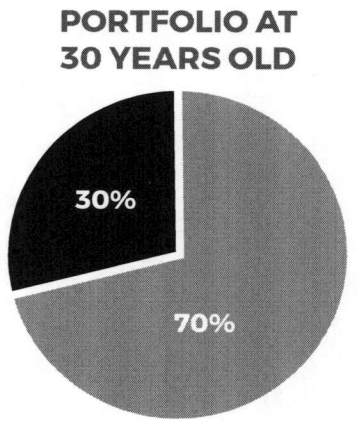

PORTFOLIO AT 30 YEARS OLD

30%

70%

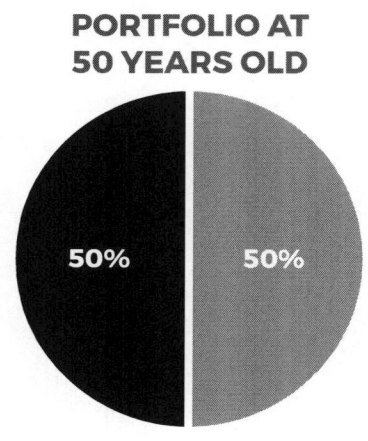

PORTFOLIO AT 50 YEARS OLD

50%

50%

investing in different asset classes. It is a little more complicated than that, but that is the basic difference between the two approaches.

Strategic asset allocation suggests that you subtract the person's age from 100. The result should be how much they should have invested in stocks. For instance, a 30-year-old should have 70% of their portfolio invested in stocks and 30% in bonds. A 50-year-old should have 50% in stocks and 50% in bonds and a 70-year-old should have 30% invested in stocks and 70% in bonds. It is a little more complicated than that, but that is the basic principle of it.

Tactical asset allocation is far more complicated. With tactical allocation, investors adjust their allocations based on market valuations. If you think stocks are going to outperform bonds, you increase your allocation to stocks. If you think foreign stocks are going to outperform domestic stocks, you increase your allocation to foreign stocks and decrease your allocation to domestic equities.

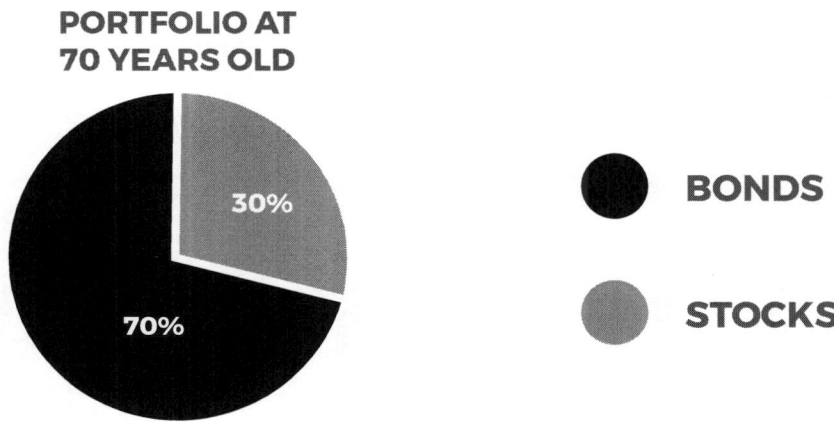

PORTFOLIO AT 70 YEARS OLD

30%

70%

● BONDS

● STOCKS

REAL DAILY

A combination of the two styles can make sense for some investors. There are times when a 50-year-old should have more than 50% invested in stocks and times when 50% might be too much. When stocks are overbought or when investor optimism is too high, it probably makes sense to lower the stock allocation across all age groups. Market tops tend to occur when investors are overly optimistic. Conversely, markets tend to bottom when investors are the most pessimistic. So if stocks are oversold and investors are extremely pessimistic, a 50-year-old would be well served to increase his or her stock allocation. In fact, even a 70-year-old would probably benefit from increasing a stock allocation at a time like that.

TAX IMPACT

A tactical asset allocation strategy can have more of an impact on taxes than a strategic one normally would. A tactical strategy has a greater chance of creating short-term capital gains due to making changes to the portfolio based on market conditions. It could also create losses that can offset gains if the investor so chooses. Because strategic asset allocation is based on age, it is far less likely to create short-term capital gains or losses. The tax consequences are something that should be taken in to account. These tax consequences are less of a concern in a qualified retirement account because the gains and losses have no impact on taxes until the assets are withdrawn from the account.

OTHER FACTORS TO CONSIDER

Your asset allocation and your portfolio management should not be a static thing. It also isn't a one-size-fits-all idea. Each investor has their own sense of how much risk they are willing to take on for a certain amount of return. One investor is willing to take a 100% loss for the chance to earn a gain of 600% or more. Others are only comfortable putting their money in ultra-safe insured certificates of deposit (CDs) or Treasuries. These are extreme examples, but there are many layers of portfolio strategies between. The idea is to find one that works for you and adjust it as you age and according to market conditions.

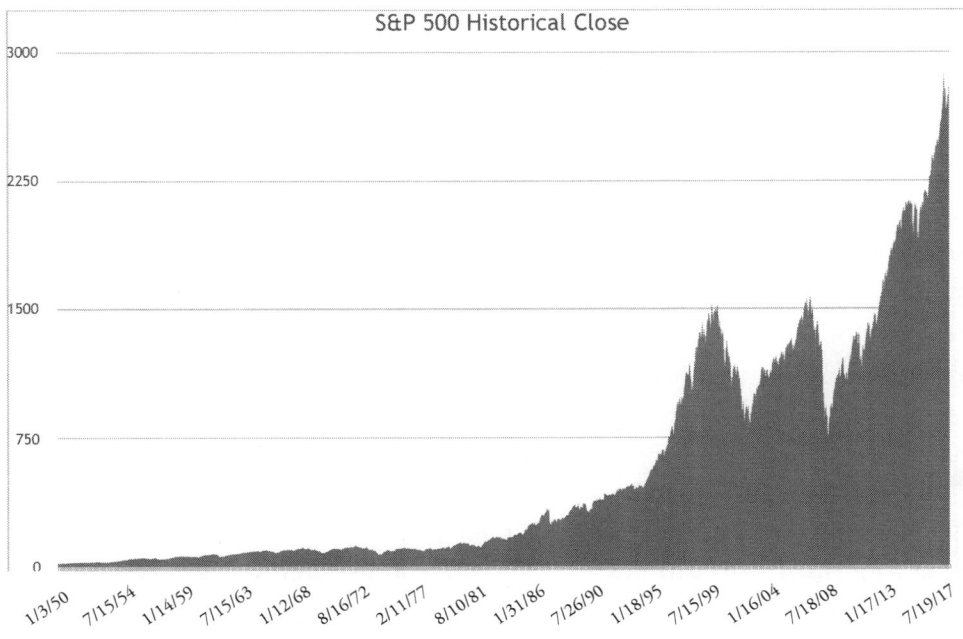

RELATIVE STRENGTH INDEX

Percent Bullish

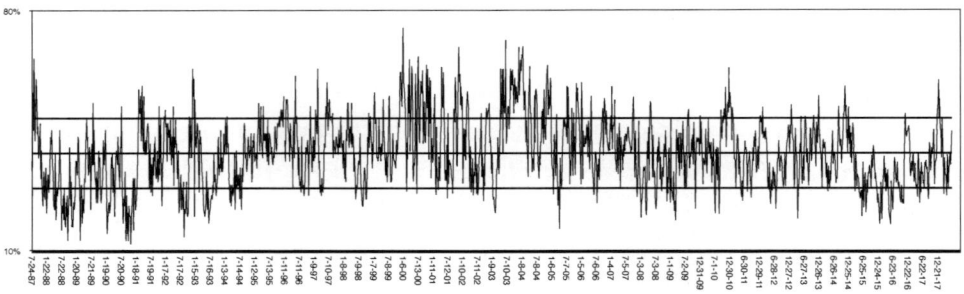

Investor sentiment and market conditions should play a role in your portfolio changes. In 2000 and again in 2007, the overall market was overbought and investor sentiment was extremely bullish. In both instances, the market dropped sharply. If an investor didn't make any changes to their portfolio, he paid a high price. At the bottoms in 2002 and 2009, the market was oversold and investors were extremely pessimistic. Investors of all ages could have boosted their returns by increasing their stock allocations at these times.

How do you know if the market is overbought or oversold? There are hundreds of different indicators that measure how overbought or oversold a stock or a market is. One of the most popular ones is the relative strength index or RSI. For long-term investors and for your retirement accounts, consider using a 10-month RSI. That is the reference point used for 2000 and 2007 as well as 2002 and 2009 in the example just mentioned.

For determining whether stocks are overly loved or not, there are also numerous sentiment indicators. There aren't as many as the overbought/oversold indicators, but there are still enough of them that you can use them to get a feel for overall investor sentiment.

Some of the more popular sentiment indicators are the Investors Intelligence Sentiment Survey, the AAII Sentiment Survey and Consumer Confidence.

The key to using these tools is to make adjustments to your portfolio accordingly. You aren't trying to time the exact top or the exact bottom. You just want to look at them from time to time and make slight adjustments. If the market is overbought, maybe lower your allocation to stocks by 5% to 10%. If it is overbought and the sentiment is extremely bullish, maybe you drop the allocation in stocks by 10% to 20%.

In 2002 or 2009, you wouldn't have wanted to shift from a 30% allocation in stocks to an 80% allocation in stocks. Again, you aren't trying to time the bottom. You are trying to avoid the deep drops associated with bear markets and trying to take advantage of the opportunities when the market is primed to outperform historical returns.

TAX IMPACT

Making adjustments to your portfolio outside of a qualified retirement account will always have an impact on your taxes. Whether you are selling a security at a loss or a gain, it will either increase your taxes or help lower your taxes. Sometimes the tax consequences will be big and at other times they will be minimal. Either way, they should certainly be part of the decision-making process. For instance, if you are worried about the market dropping and want to lower your stock exposure, you will want to consider how long you have held the stock or funds. Let's say you have two very similar holdings. One has been in your account for a couple of years and the other one has only been in your account for a few months. The one is a long-term holding and the other is a short-term holding. If all other things are equal, you would want to sell the long-term holding before the short-term holding.

CHAPTER 2.
INVESTING BEFORE THE AGE OF 40

Few people under the age of 40 are really worried about their tax situation in retirement. Most people in their 20s aren't even worried about retirement, let alone the tax situation when they get there. But the fact is most people start investing in their 20s and 30s in an employee-sponsored retirement plan—usually a 401(k) or 403(b). For the purposes of this book, we'll say 401(k) throughout to mean any tax-deferred workplace retirement plan that relies on employee contributions.

When you first start investing for retirement it is usually some random choices between a bunch of mutual funds. There is little thought put into the decisions and there is also very little guidance on which funds to choose. Very few 401(k) sponsors provide any insights in to what funds employees should invest in. And that is because they don't want that responsibility. Hopefully this book will help a few people in this area.

When you are in your 20s and 30s, that's when you should be the most aggressive with your investments. Why is that? Because if the market goes through a bearish period while you are under 40, you still have a lot of time to make up the losses before you will need your money.

If you were 25 in 2000 and mostly invested in stocks in your 401(k), you took some serious losses. But even if you stayed with the same funds and didn't make any adjustments, you were likely much better off well before 2007. The reasons are twofold: The market recovered, for one, and by continuing to invest a portion of each paycheck you were dollar-cost averaging into your investments at a lower price.

THE BENEFITS OF DOLLAR-COST AVERAGING

If you aren't familiar with the term "dollar-cost averaging," it simply means that you make a set dollar amount purchase at regular intervals. By doing this, you buy more shares when the price of the fund is down and fewer shares when the price is up.

It's counterintuitive, but dollar-cost averaging is a great strategy, so long as you stick with it. As an example of dollar-cost averaging, let's look at the SPDR S&P 500 ETF (NYSE: SPY). You will hear this ETF called the Spyders and it is one of the most heavily traded ETFs there is. It was the first U.S.-based ETF and it replicates the performance of the S&P 500, the broad index of large U.S. stocks.

At the peak in 2000, the Spyders were at $111. If you were contributing $25 each month, you would have been buying a little over two shares per month. At the low in 2002, the Spyders were under $60 and you would have been buying just over four shares per month. It thus took until November 2006 for the ETF to make it back above the $111 mark.

It took the Spyders 80 months to get back above the $111 mark, and that includes dividends. By dollar-cost averaging, if you bought three shares per month on average, you would accumulate 240 shares worth $26,640. You would have invested $20,000 (80 x 250) over the years but have 33% more money.

By the same token, a person that bought 240 shares at the high in March 2000 would simply be at break-even on their investment in November 2006.

That is the benefit of dollar-cost averaging. Now consider what happened from 2007 through 2010. Once again we saw the Spyders drop sharply in value. It took until January 2011 for the ETF to get back above $111.

If you were 25 in 2000 and continued investing in the Spyders on a monthly basis, you were able to make a decent return. If you made a one-time purchase in 2000, you broke even over those almost 11 years. And you are now only 36 years old. Plenty of time left to invest! If you were 50 in 2000 and made a one-time purchase of the Spyders in an IRA, however, your investment made nothing.

This is why being aggressive and making regular contributions when you are young is so important. It allows you to make up for losses well before you reach retirement age and to benefit from buying shares at a low price to average out your costs.

Perhaps most importantly, dollar-cost averaged short-circuits our very human response to falling investment values. We tend to want to buy more of an investment as it rises, imaging only even higher prices. When prices fall, we typically get depressed and stop buying or even try to sell.

In fact, the opposite reaction is the more powerful response. Slowing down your buying when prices rise conserves cash for better pricing. Buying more as prices fall means getting more shares, which then usually recover in price and add to return. It's as simple as "buy low and sell high," yet most people literally do the opposite. Dollar-cost averaging enforces the right behavior regardless of how we feel about the investment's value at any given moment.

REAL DAILY

401k Plan Limits for Year	2018	2017	2016	2015	2014	2013	2012
401k Elective Deferrals	$18,500	$18,000	$18,000	$18,000	$17,500	$17,500	$17,000
Annual Defined Contribution Limit	$55,000	$54,000	$53,000	$53,000	$52,000	$51,000	$50,000
Annual Compensation Limit	$275,000	$270,000	$265,000	$265,000	$260,000	$255,000	$250,000
Catch-Up Contribution Limit	$6,000	$6,000	$6,000	$6,000	$5,500	$5,500	$5,500
Highly Compensated Employees	$120,000	$120,000	$120,000	$120,000	$115,000	$115,000	$115,000
Non-401k Related Limits							
403b/457 Elective Deferrals	$18,500	$18,000	$18,000	$18,000	$17,500	$17,500	$17,000
SIMPLE Employee Deferrals	$12,500	$12,500	$12,500	$12,500	$12,000	$12,000	$11,500
SIMPLE Catch-Up Deferral	$3,000	$3,000	$3,000	$3,000	$2,500	$2,500	$2,500
SEP Minimum Compensation	$600	$600	$600	$600	$550	$550	$550
SEP Annual Compensation Limit	$275,000	$270,000	$265,000	$265,000	$260,000	$255,000	$250,000
Social Security Wage Base	$128,400	$127,200	$118,500	$118,500	$117,000	$113,700	$110,100

TAX IMPACT

When you make a contribution to your retirement account, you are allowed to reduce your income on your tax returns by the amount of the contribution. The contributions can be made to employer-sponsored plans or to an Individual Retirement Account (IRA). The contributions lower your income tax during your working years whether you are in your 30s or your 60s. You should consider maxing out the allowable retirement contributions before investing in a non-retirement account.

A CLEARER DEFINITION OF 'AGGRESSIVE' INVESTMENTS

The idea of being aggressive is a central part of this section about investing when you are young. A clearer definition of what defines aggressive investments is probably warranted at this time.

There are pecking orders for the risk level between asset classes and you can also rank investments within each asset class. Government bonds are some of the least risky investments. But bonds issued by the governments of more developed countries such as the United States or Germany are far less risky than countries such as Argentina or Venezuela, where governments often are in turmoil.

Municipal bonds can be broken down by risk as well. State issued bonds are generally considered safer than bonds issued by an individual city. The higher level of authority and taxing power is part of the reason.

If you were to rank the asset classes in order from least risky to most risky, it would look something like this:

• Money Market and certificates of deposit (CDs)

• Government Bonds

• Corporate Bonds

• Stocks

As was mentioned before, you can then take each of these asset classes and do another layer of risk evaluation. For bonds, you have the ratings from Moody's and S&P to help evaluate risk.

When it comes to stocks, there are many different factors to be evaluated. You have the size of the company, the industry the company is in, the age of the company and so on. There are too many to list in their entirety here, but let's take a look at a few.

For one, large-cap stocks are less risky than mid-cap or small-cap. Consumer staples stocks are considered less risky than the other sectors and serve as a safe harbor during occasional market corrections.

The reason for the sector evaluations is due to several factors. The historical volatility of the sectors is certainly one of those factors. Utilities and consumer staples tend to be less volatile. If you look at the two bearish cycles we have seen so far in this century (2000-2002 and 2007-2009), the consumer staples sector dropped the least during both of those bear markets.

One reason why is that demand for the products and services provided by utility companies and consumer staples companies tends to be fairly constant (food and home heating). During recessionary periods in the economy, the demand for consumer discretionary products and technology companies (your Netflix subscription, for instance, or a new iPhone) can vary greatly compared to when the economy was expanding. This contributes to the volatility difference between the sectors.

While the consumer staples sector did drop less during the two bearish periods, it has also lagged behind during the huge rally since the last bear market. From the lows in March 2009 through the end of April 2017, the Consumer Staples Select Sector SPDR (XLP) gained 229% while the S&P 500 SPDR (SPY) gained 364%. The ETFs that represent the more volatile sectors, such as consumer discretionary, financials and technology, have all outpaced the S&P 500 Index. The Consumer Discretionary Select Sector SPDR (XLY) gained more than 627% during that period.

This is where you have to look at market conditions and your risk-tolerance level to make adjustments to your portfolio. It is also why the early part of your retirement planning is so important. If you had started investing in the XLY with systematic purchases at the top in 2007 you would have experienced a big loss by the bottom in 2009. The shares dropped by more than half!

But if you were young and knew you had time to make up the losses, you would have been rewarded greatly by patiently investing over the next nine years.

By the same token, an older investor could have avoided a fair amount of the downturn in 2009 by lowering their equity allocations significantly before the decline. The warning signs were there with an overbought market and heavily optimistic investor sentiment.

Regardless of your age, there are always going to be periods where the market is offering greater opportunity or offering a greater threat than usual. The trick is not to turn off risk but to minimize it appropriately in order to avoid making an emotional decision that costs you big money down the line.

TAX IMPACT

There is another benefit to being more aggressive with the investments in your retirement accounts. Because the growth of a retirement account isn't taxed, it is a better place to make more aggressive trades. Not necessarily option trades or buying penny stocks, but buying high-growth ETFs and mutual funds makes more sense. The account grows tax-free until you start taking distributions. The average person sees their tax bracket drop when they hit retirement.

BUILDING YOUR PORTFOLIO AT 30

Let's look at how you could build a portfolio at the age of 30. The model is based on market conditions being normal. This means it isn't overbought and the optimism isn't too high. It also means the market isn't oversold or hated.

To build the portfolio, you can use the strategic asset allocation theory. You will want a 70% allocation to stock-based investments and a 30% allocation to bond-based investments.

You are moderately tolerant of risk and intend to retire at 65. This gives you 35 years until you intend to start taking distributions from your retirement account. This is the time to be as aggressive as you are comfortable being. Now is the time to divide your stock portfolio between funds that focus on growth. Some of these areas are emerging market funds, small-cap funds, technology funds and consumer discretionary funds. There is very little need for you to be investing in utility funds, consumer staples funds or large-cap funds.

You can be more aggressive even within the fixed-income portion of your portfolio. Instead of investing in U.S. government bonds, look at investing in funds that invest in emerging market bonds. Other aggressive fixed-income funds you can consider are high-yield corporate funds, sometimes called "junk" bonds. Unless the stock market is extremely overbought and optimism is high, Treasuries shouldn't even be a concern here. And municipal bond funds should never be bought within a retirement account. There isn't any point. Municipals pay lower yields because the income isn't taxed but in a tax-deferred plan you are already shielded from taxes. Go ahead and get the higher yield from corporate bonds.

It's worth repeating that you want to be as aggressive as you can in the early years of your retirement investing, given normal market conditions. Even if the market is overbought and the optimism is high, if you are 30 you shouldn't really drop below a 50% allocation to stocks. Remember, your contributions are being made on a regular basis and the dollar-cost averaging will help offset some of the losses as the market drops. You get to buy low over and over.

If the market is oversold and there is excessive pessimism towards the market, you should bump up your equity allocations to even higher than the 70% level. This would represent an opportunity for you to grow your portfolio even faster. You don't have to get the timing exactly right. You have time on your side and you are making regular contributions, and that's what matters decades down the line.

TAX IMPACT

This may seem obvious, but the more you are able to grow your portfolio in the early years, the better off you will be in retirement. You can maximize the growth you experience early on by taking advantage of opportunities and by knowing you have time on your side, especially in tax-deferred accounts. Be more aggressive than you will be in later years. When you reach retirement and are focused on investing for income, the amount you have to invest will determine how much you get in return.

REAL DAILY

CHAPTER 3.
THE MIDDLE YEARS OF WORK, INVESTING AND RETIREMENT PLANNING

When you enter your 40s, several things happen that will impact your retirement plans. First of all, statistics show that most people see their earnings peak and flatten out during their 40s. This is the period when you transition from being closer to the beginning of your career to being closer to the end of your career. This is also the time when you transition from being focused on growing your portfolio to a combination of growing and protecting your portfolio.

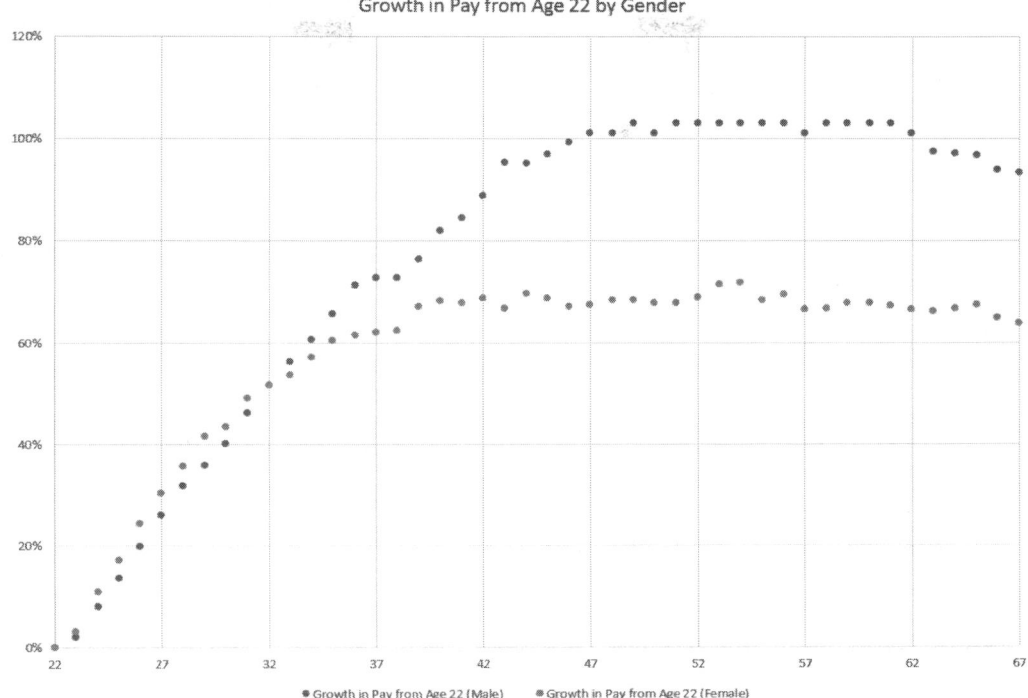

Growth in Pay from Age 22 by Gender

● Growth in Pay from Age 22 (Male)　　● Growth in Pay from Age 22 (Female)

Unlike the first stage of investing toward retirement, during the second stage time isn't on your side as much as it used to be. If you are in your late 40s going through a bearish cycle in the stock market, it can wreak havoc on your portfolio if you aren't careful.

This whole period of your life is about transitions. At work you are likely no longer one of the young people but rather you are one of the seasoned veterans. In your home life, if you are a parent you will likely transition from having your kids under your roof to having them move out. Your investment plan will also need to go through a transition during this phase of your life, too.

THE TRANSITION PHASE OF YOUR RETIREMENT PLANNING

In the first phase of your investing toward retirement, the focus should be on growth. In the second phase, the focus has to shift to a balanced approach. We still need for the portfolio to grow, but part of the focus needs to shift to protecting what you have already saved.

The good news is that you will likely make more money during this phase of your life than at any other point. This means that you have more to contribute to your retirement accounts and you will have more disposable income. At least that is how it works for the majority of people.

During this phase—age 40 to 50—it is likely that you will open a regular investment account for additional investing outside of your retirement accounts. At first it may seem like this account should be treated differently than your retirement accounts, but it is still part of the total portfolio. You need to include all accounts as part of the total retirement picture.

That being said, investments within your retirement account and those outside of your retirement account can be handled differently to minimize or reduce taxes. For instance, the most aggressive portion of the overall portfolio should be held inside your 401(k) or IRA. Why? Because they are most likely to generate the greatest returns and if they are in a retirement account they don't get taxed—yet.

Even if you have short-term gains, if they are in a retirement account they don't generate additional taxes for you. And remember you are likely in the highest tax bracket you will ever be in during this phase of your life. By having the investments with the greatest growth potential in your retirement accounts, you reduce the taxes generated in the current year.

In the regular, non-retirement account, such as a brokerage account at Fidelity or E-Trade, you can invest in longer term investments that are less likely to create short-term gains or losses. You should put your more conservative investments in this account. The more conservative investments are also less likely to experience big gains and unexpectedly bump you up to a higher tax bracket.

If you are starting to look at municipal bonds to generate additional income without generating additional taxes, they should be in the brokerage account. There isn't any benefit to investing in municipal bonds inside a retirement account since the bonds aren't taxed like other sources of income and since the gains inside the retirement accounts aren't taxed at this time.

TAX IMPACT

Viewing your retirement accounts and any regular investment accounts as one big portfolio can help you balance your overall portfolio. It can also give you ways to minimize your current tax liability. By keeping your investments with the greatest growth potential inside your retirement account, you can still keep the focus on growth for this portion. The taxes on the gains won't be due until you start taking distributions from the retirement accounts.

THE 40/60 TARGET PORTFOLIO

Staying with the strategic asset allocation model, this is the phase where your portfolio will become more balanced between stocks and bonds. Of course, there are many other asset classes besides these two, such as real estate, precious metals, even cash. But for the purposes of this book and this chapter, we will stay focused on these two major asset classes.

Again, you will want to keep market conditions in mind and make adjustments accordingly. If market conditions are in the normal range, the stock allocation will range from 50% to 60%. If market conditions show that the market is oversold and there is a lot of pessimism toward stocks, you should consider bumping up the stock allocation by 10% to 20%. (That's right, increase your holdings. People are selling so you should be buying!) If the market is overbought and there is too much optimism, you should consider dropping the stock allocation by 10% to 20%. (Now the opposite holds: If everyone is a buyer, be a seller.)

TARGET PORTFOLIO

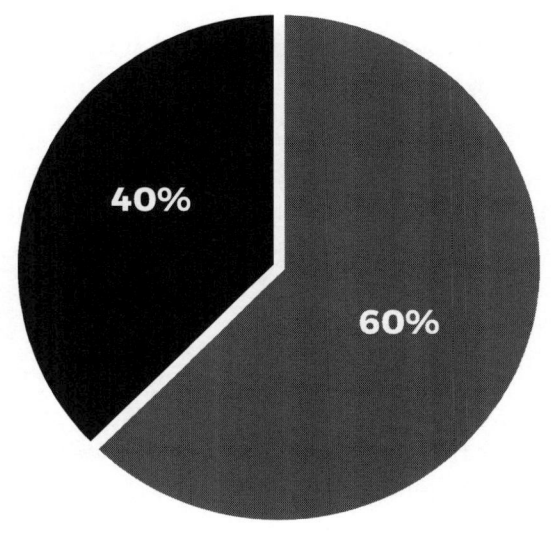

 **BONDS**    **STOCKS**

In Chapter 2, the sample portfolio was built with a 30-year-old in mind. It represented the middle of the age range from 20 to 40 or so. This time, the portfolio will be built with a 45-year-old in mind. Once again, the middle of the age range, from 40 to 50.

In addition to dialing back the equity allocation to 55%, you will want to change the allocation to the types of stocks you focus on. In the first stage of your investing for retirement, the focus should be on growth. In this stage, you still want growth but you also want safety. Instead of putting the entire stock allocation in technology, emerging market and small-cap stocks, you will want to lower those allocations now. These assets should be redistributed to less volatile investments and ones that still offer growth possibilities.

For instance, you may have had 15% allocated to fast-growing, more volatile small-cap funds in your 20s and 30s. Now lower that exposure to between 5% and 10%. The 5% to 10% you take out of small-cap stocks can be reallocated to large-cap and mid-cap stocks—still stocks, but far less volatile shares. In the first phase of investing for retirement, you may have had 15% allocated to technology funds. Now you want to lower that to between 5% and 10% and redistribute the money to financial and industrial stocks and funds. The same thing should be done with emerging market investments. Lower the allocation to these stocks and redistribute money to developed-country foreign funds or global equity funds.

The goal here within the equity portion of your portfolio is to keep some money invested for high growth potential but lower the allocation. If there is a bear market and stocks fall or go flat for a long period, you won't have as much time to make up the losses.

You should go through the same process with the fixed-income portion of your portfolio, seeking to lower the risk and increase safety. In the first phase, you wanted to maximize the return with investments in high-yield funds and emerging market debt funds. As you did with the stock allocations, you will want to lower these allocations by 5% to 10% and add safer fixed-income investments. Investment grade corporate bond funds should enter the picture at this time, along with funds that invest in global developed-country debt instruments.

Another investment instrument that could be used during this phase of your retirement planning and investing is preferred stocks. A preferred stock is a different ownership class that has a higher priority on dividends and asset claims than common stock. Because of these higher rights, the shares are considered safer and are generally less volatile.

As with the other asset classes discussed so far, there are mutual funds and ETFs that invest in preferred stocks. The yields on preferred stocks tend to be higher than those of common stocks and higher than on corporate bonds. The growth potential isn't usually as high as common stock, but there also tends to be less downside risk should a bear market ensue.

TAX IMPACT

Preferred stocks and foreign debt could be used wisely in the portion of the portfolio outside retirement accounts. They tend to be longer-term investments with less chance of short-term gains impacting your taxes greatly. The preferred tax treatment given to corporate dividends helps. There is also the potential for a foreign tax credit for any gains and income paid to you from any investments in foreign debt and equities.

HOW TO MAKE UP FOR LOST TIME

If you are in your 40s and haven't started investing, you need to change your approach a little. You will have to be a little more aggressive than others your age and you would be wise to try to take advantage of special opportunities. If you get a chance to invest when the market is down, for instance, this can help you make up for lost time.

Using the 45-year-old scenario from above, instead of having 55% allocated to equities, you should probably look at 60%. You don't want to be drastic, but little changes can help more than you think. Getting your returns to improve by 2% to 3% over the course of several years can make a big difference in the long run.

The changes you would make to take advantage of an opportunity should also lean towards the aggressive side. The same holds true for the changes you should make if there is the threat of a market decline. Strategies to protect the downside should lean towards the more drastic to protect what you have.

Within the equity portion of your portfolio, you should keep a little more allocated to higher growth funds than you normally would. Instead of dropping from a 15% allocation in emerging market funds or tech funds to a 5% allocation, you should consider dropping to a 10% allocation.

Even the allocations within the fixed-income portion of the portfolio should be more aggressive under normal circumstances. You should maintain higher percentages of high-yield and emerging market funds than others would as you are trying to build a big enough retirement account with less time. Investment-grade bond funds and preferred stock funds can still be part of the equation, but not necessarily as big of an allocation.

You shouldn't even consider opening a non-retirement account until you have maxed-out the retirement contributions. At this time, the maximum contribution to an IRA is $5,500 for those under the age of 50. If you are married, that means you can contribute a total of $11,000 to your separate IRA accounts. You may be entitled to a full or partial deduction of your contribution on your taxes, depending upon your income. Currently, the limits are going through changes and the amount is affected if you or your spouse has a retirement plan at work.

TAX IMPACT

In order to determine if you can deduct your IRA contribution and how much is deductible comes down to several factors. One determinant is if you or your spouse is eligible for an employer-sponsored retirement plan. Your joint adjusted gross income is also a factor. Even if you can't deduct your contribution, it might still be worth making a contribution to an IRA. The assets will grow tax-free within the IRA and any gains won't impact your current tax liability.

MAX OUT YOUR SPONSORED PLAN CONTRIBUTIONS

One thing you should try to do no matter what age you are is to max out your contribution to any employer-sponsored retirement plan, such as a 401(k). First, most employers match a certain percentage of your contribution to some degree. This is free money being added to your retirement account. Secondly, even beyond the employer match, the contributions you make to a sponsored plan reduce your taxable income.

Since taxes are progressive (you are taxed more on additional dollars), reducing your income by any amount reduces your taxes that year by the most you can get, dollar for dollar. For instance, if you make $85,000 a year, then you are taxed at 24% for the $2,500 above the $82,500 threshold for that bracket. You would owe Uncle Sam $600.

Save at least $2,500 a year and the taxes on those dollars is zero, not 24%. You owe nothing on that income for this year. Meanwhile, the dollars below the threshold are already taxed at 22%. Save another $2,500 and you pay nothing instead of $550 on that money.

According to Investopedia, the most common company match is 50 cents on the dollar. This means that for every dollar you contribute to your 401(k), the company adds another 50 cents. This can be an unlimited match in dollars, theoretically, but in practice about 40%

of companies make a 50% match up to 6% of the employee's pay. From that same research, 38% of companies match dollar for dollar up to 3% of the employee's pay. Either way, the employer contribution boosts how much you have in your retirement account with no additional saving on your part.

For example, if you make $85,000 and save 6%, that's $5,100. The company adds $2,550, so your total contribution comes to $7,650. The great news is that any corporate matching you get is not counted against annual contribution limits. There's literally no reason not to save at least enough to get the free company money, and saving the maximum doesn't hurt either—you still get the matching dollars.

CURRENT TAX BRACKETS

RATE	FOR UNMARRIED INDIVIDUALS, TAXABLE INCOME OVER
10%	$0
12%	$9,525
22%	$38,700
24%	$82,500
32%	$157,500
35%	$200,000
37%	$500,000

RATE	FOR MARRIED INDIVIDUALS FILING JOINT RETURNS, TAXABLE INCOME OVER
10%	$0
12%	$19,050
22%	$77,400
24%	$165,000
32%	$315,000
35%	$400,000
37%	$600,000

RATE	FOR HEADS OF HOUSEHOLDS, TAXABLE INCOME OVER
10%	$0
12%	$13,600
22%	$51,800
24%	$82,500
32%	$157,500
35%	$200,000
37%	$500,000

HOW MUCH CAN I CONTRIBUTE?

At this time, employees may contribute a maximum of $18,500 per year to a 401(k). This amount was increased for 2018. Even if the employer only matches up to 6% of your income, the contributions are made pre-tax and thus lower your earned income on your W2. This automatically lowers your tax liability. If you qualify, you can still potentially make a contribution to an IRA and get another deduction. But you will want to check out the limitations on IRA deductions from the Internal Revenue Service.

The biggest downside to making a maximum contribution to your 401(k) is that you can be limited to certain group of funds from the plan sponsor. In other words, you have less flexibility than you would have with an IRA (though much higher annual contribution limits).

TYPE OF ACCOUNT	2018 LIMIT	LIMIT IF 50 OR OLDER	INCOME LIMIT (MARRIED)
401(k)	$18,500	$18,500	DETERMINED BY IRS
IRA	$5,500	$6,500	$189,000 OR LESS
Roth IRA	$5,500	$6,500	$189,000 OR LESS
Roth 401(k)	$18,500	$18,500	NONE

If you are eligible for the deduction and the funds in your sponsored plan are less desirable, an IRA contribution could be a better option for you. It was pointed out earlier that most sponsored plans use mutual funds rather than ETFs. Mutual funds tend to have higher management fees than ETFs and that ultimately has an impact on your returns. There has been a small shift in sponsored plans with more of them using ETFs instead of mutual funds, so it's worth checking out in advance.

TAX IMPACT

Contributing to a sponsored plan has several positive impacts on your retirement plans. As was mentioned, the match offered by most employers is an immediate boost to your return. If you contribute $3,000 and just put it in a savings account earning 1%, the $1,500 contributed by your employer amounts to a 50% return for you. Secondly, the contributions to the sponsored plan reduce your income in the year the contribution was made and that lowers your current tax liability. There is also the benefit that the money is growing tax-free until you start taking distributions.

REAL DAILY

CHAPTER 4.
INVESTING FOR RETIREMENT IN YOUR 50s

Turning 50 can be a big event in your life. Even though it is just a number, it represents a turning point in many ways. If you and your spouse have kids, this is the decade where you are most likely to become empty-nesters. It is also the decade where you see a shift in your investing for retirement. This is the point where your investments, under normal conditions, should shift to having more fixed-income investments than equity investments.

The term "normal conditions" is used throughout this book. It means that the market isn't overbought or oversold and the sentiment isn't overly optimistic or pessimistic.

As for market indications, you can use something as simple as the 10-month Relative Strength Index (RSI) on the S&P 500 to determine whether the overall market is overbought or oversold.

The RSI is a very common indicator and it also seems to be pretty accurate. There will be an entire section about special circumstances in the last chapter, so don't worry about learning this just yet if you don't already know how to use it.

Getting a read on the sentiment is a little more difficult, but not so difficult that you will have trouble finding it at any time. Two of the better sentiment indicators are the Investors Intelligence Sentiment Survey and the Consumer Confidence Index from the Conference Board. Again, there will be more information about these indicators in the last chapter.

For now, let's focus on the decade of your 50s and how things change.

PROTECTING YOUR PORTFOLIO BECOMES MORE IMPORTANT THAN GROWTH

When you enter your 50s, if you plan to retire at 65 you now only have 15 years to prepare. If the market goes through a major bearish phase over those 15 years or some part of them, you won't have nearly as long to be patient and wait for it to recover.

As an example, consider what an investor who was 50 in 2000 would have gone through. The S&P dropped approximately 50% from the high in 2000 to the low in 2002. If someone bought at the high and held on, the index now has to climb 100% for them to break even.

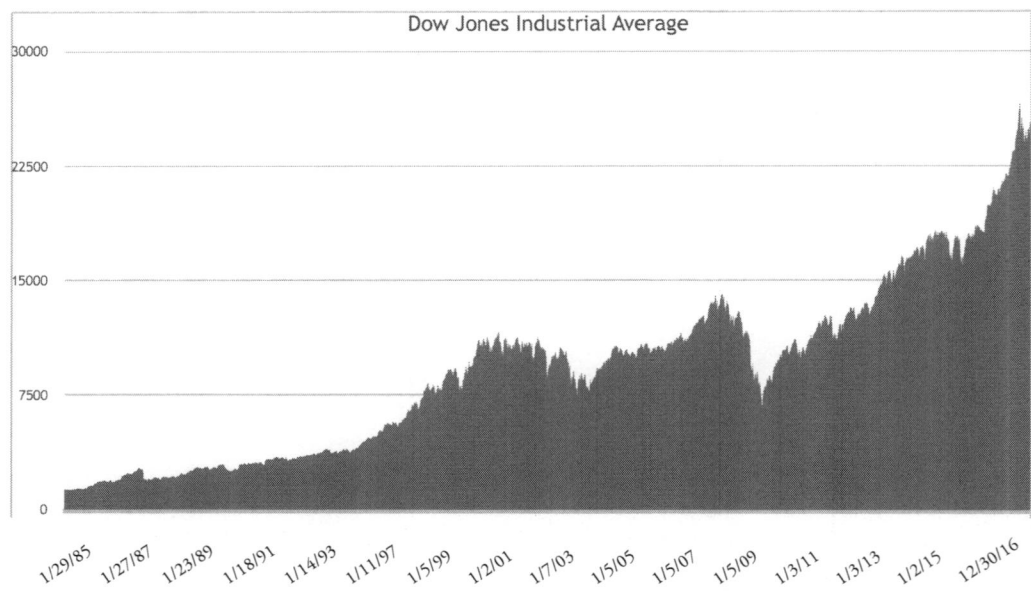

The index did that, but not until 2007. Then the index dropped over 50% from the 2007 high to the 2009 low. If that same investor that bought the S&P in 2000 was still holding on, they now had to wait until 2013 before they saw a significant profit. Can you imagine waiting 13 years to see a profit? Probably not.

Yes, this is an extreme example, but it is certainly possible. This is why you have to make changes to your allocations and why you want to pay attention to special circumstances. The S&P 500 Index, an index of large-cap U.S. stocks, was overbought in 2000 and again in 2007. The sentiment was extremely optimistic in 2000 and again in 2007. Investors who didn't make changes with that knowledge likely experienced heavy losses.

The following table was created with different allocation amounts to help you see how much of a difference this can make in your results. The five-year period chosen was from January 2007 through January 2012. In order to simplify things, two ETFs were chosen that represent stocks and bonds. The SPDR S&P 500 ETF (SPY) represents stocks and the iShares 20+ Year Treasury Bond ETF (TLT) represents bonds, in this case government bonds.

70/30 Portfolio	SPY Value	TLT Value	Total Value
1/1/17	$ 70,000.00	$ 30,000.00	$ 100,000.00
3/5/09	$ 35,533.57	$ 38,920.02	$ 74,453.59
1/1/02	$ 69,032.72	$ 50,272.92	$ 119,305.63
50/50 Portfolio	SPY Value	TLT Value	Total Value
1/1/17	$ 50,000.00	$ 50,000.00	$ 100,000.00
3/5/09	$ 25,381.01	$ 64,866.44	$ 90,247.44
1/1/02	$ 49,308.87	$ 83,787.85	$ 133,096.72
30/70 Portfolio	SPY Value	TLT Value	Total Value
1/1/17	$ 30,000.00	$ 70,000.00	$ 100,000.00
3/5/09	$ 15,228.60	$ 90,812.85	$ 106,041.45
1/1/02	$ 29,585.32	$ 117,302.79	$ 146,888.11

There are three portfolios represented and no changes were made to the allocations during the five-year period. The 70/30 portfolio represents a 70% allocation to stocks and 30% to bonds. The 50/50 portfolio has 50% in stocks and 50% in bonds. The 30/70 portfolio has 30% in stocks and 70% in bonds.

What you see is that as the market went through the bearish phase and then a recovery, the 30/70 portfolio (mostly bonds) outperformed the other two portfolios by a wide margin. Now imagine being 55 years old and having a 70/30 allocation (mostly stocks) and seeing your account down by more than 25% at the bottom, in March 2009.

This is one period of time where being more conservative with your allocations would have paid off in a big way. This isn't meant to suggest that anyone should use these exact allocation changes. It is simply meant to illustrate how big of a difference allocation can make to the end result—your retirement balance.

It should be mentioned, too, that both the SPY and TLT results include the dividends paid out over the time period. Obviously the dividends for the TLT—bond interest payments, in effect—were a big reason investors used that particular ETF. In this case, the fund was meant to protect against a drop in the stock market.

This next table shows how you could have benefitted from a more tactical strategy by increasing your stock allocation toward the end of the bear market. The table assumes the same time frame as the table above, but the portfolio starts with a 30/70 allocation and shifts to a 70/30 allocation in January 2009 when the S&P was hitting oversold territory.

Tactical Portfolio	SPY Value	TLT Value	Total Value
30/70 balance 1/1/07	$ 30,000.00	$ 70,000.00	$ 100,000.00
70/30 balance 1/2/09	$ 20,575.02	$ 100,110.97	$ 120,685.99
Value on 1/1/12 before rebalance to 50/50	$ 121,476.65	$ 42,423.24	$ 163,899.89

Again, this table isn't meant to suggest that this is how anyone in particular changed their actual allocations. It is only meant to show how taking advantage of special opportunities could impact your end result. January 1, 2009 was not the bottom in the S&P; the bottom came a couple of months later. But, by 2012, there was a $17,000 difference between this portfolio and the best return from the static, non-tactical portfolios. The difference between this portfolio and the worst-performing portfolio from above is $45,594. That is a huge difference in your retirement funds!

Hopefully, these tables have helped you understand the importance of allocations and how big of a difference small adjustments can make. Obviously, the time period used in the tables is an extreme example as it included one of the worst bear markets in history, but that is the point. The need to protect your portfolio as you get closer to retirement age is every bit as important as it is to grow your portfolio.

DIALING BACK THE AGGRESSIVENESS OF YOUR PORTFOLIO

Now that you have seen some examples of what can happen, let's look at what changes you will want to make to your portfolio. The obvious goal during your 50s is to reduce the volatility of your portfolio—how much its value moves up and down in response to the economy and the stock market itself.

The most obvious move is that you shift the allocation to having more fixed-income investments than equity investments during normal market conditions. In addition to that move, you should also be shifting the investments within the two parts of the portfolio. In the chapter about investing before 40, the bulk of the assets in the equity portion of the portfolio were invested in high-growth funds. Now that you are in your 50s, very little should be in high-growth funds.

Instead of investing in tech funds, emerging market funds, and small and mid-cap funds—all growth-oriented—your focus should now be on more stable funds. Sectors such as consumer staples, industrials and utilities tend to be less volatile. Domestic large-cap funds and global large-cap funds tend to be more stable than small-cap or emerging market funds.

At this point, your allocations to high-growth funds should not represent more than 10% to 15% of the total allocation in the equity portion. And that is a total allocation to all growth funds. Another 20% to 25% can be allocated to the middle range of the risk hierarchy—mid-cap funds, maybe some energy and financial funds.

The remaining allocation, 60% to 75%, should be in the less volatile funds, large-cap stock funds such as the SPDR S&P 500 ETF (SPY) mentioned above. The SPY tends to be less volatile, for instance, than the PowerShares QQQ ETF (QQQ). The QQQ represents the Nasdaq 100 index. You could consider allocations to global funds that focus on investments in stocks in developed countries over emerging markets.

The bond portion of the portfolio should also be changed with less risk in mind. You can still have a small portion allocated to high-yield funds and emerging market debt funds, but the allocation shouldn't be more than 25%. Another 30% to 40% could be allocated to foreign debt in developed countries and investment-grade corporate bonds. Finally, the remaining portion could be allocated to government bond funds. TLT was used in the tables above and it falls into this category. TLT represents long-term bonds, but there are also short-term government bond funds and intermediate bond funds.

The main idea of your allocation changes here is to protect the downside. Unless there is a special circumstance where the market is oversold and the pessimism is high, protecting the portfolio is more important than growth at this time.

TAX IMPACT

At this point, any and all equity portions of the overall portfolio should be held in retirement accounts. The potential capital gains of those funds can still grow tax-free and not create taxable events. If you have equity investments outside of the retirement accounts, they should be the least aggressive ones. The last thing you want is to have a high-growth fund shoot up in a regular account and create a capital gain that bumps you up to a higher tax bracket. It is nice to get big capital gains, but it is better if they happen inside the retirement accounts where they aren't taxed.

REAL DAILY

OTHER CHANGES THAT HAPPEN NOW THAT YOU'RE 50

Besides the allocation changes you should make, there are other changes that happen when you hit 50. You can make your own jokes here about what happens to the body after you hit 50, but the changes you need to focus on most regard contribution limits.

The maximum IRA contribution goes from $5,500 to $6,500 when you turn 50. The IRS allows this so that people that haven't contributed enough to their retirement accounts can catch up. Even if you are on track with your retirement planning, you would be wise to make the maximum contribution in order to get any deduction you may be eligible for and to add to your tax-advantaged investments.

The maximum contribution to a 401(k) also goes up. In this instance, the maximum employee contribution goes from $18,500 to $24,500. This happens in the year you turn 50, so even if your birthday isn't until November or December, you can start making these additional contributions in January of the year you turn 50. You would be wise to contribute as much as you can in order to lower your current tax liability and to get as much of your money growing tax-free.

If you own your own business, there are additional options for you that can really help you catch up on your retirement savings. Instead of a traditional IRA or Roth IRA, you can consider a SIMPLE IRA or a Simplified Employee Pension (SEP IRA). The contribution limits on these retirement accounts are considerably higher than the traditional IRA or Roth IRA.

The term SIMPLE IRA stands for Savings Incentive Match Plan for Employees. If you are self-employed, you can put 100% of your net earnings, up to $12,500, from self-employment into a SIMPLE IRA. If you are over 50, that contribution limit jumps by $3,000 to $15,500. Plus, you can match your contribution by another 3% as the employer.

SEP IRA contributions are even higher than the SIMPLE IRA. For 2018, self-employed people can contribute up to 25% of their earnings up to a limit of $55,000. You can make contributions to a SEP IRA and a traditional IRA as well. So, if you have the means, you could contribute up to 25% of your income or $55,000 to your SEP IRA plan and an additional $6,500 if you are over 50. Adding those two together, we get $61,500 being contributed to your retirement accounts with tax advantages possible from every bit of it.

A third kind of retirement plan, new on the scene, is the solo 401(k). This is exactly what it sounds like. You are creating a personal 401(k) plan as part of your business with the same limits of normal, corporate-world 401(k): $18,500 and $24,500 for those 50 and over. In addition, you can set aside 25% of net income.

You don't need an LLC or other corporate structure to use these plans, just income from a business, even if it's a side business. Obviously, you can't contribute to a workplace plan plus a personal plan, but the upside is that you don't need a company plan if you are self-employed; all you need is to file normal taxes as a sole proprietor.

TAX IMPACT

Most people make more money in their 50s than at any other point in their lives. It is a great time, if you have the means, to contribute as much as you possibly can towards retirement. This will help you reduce the taxable income as you are making the most money. At this point, you are likely losing deductions as your children leave the house or reach an age where you are no longer allowed to count them as a dependent. Maxing out your retirement contributions can offset the loss of the dependent child deduction.

CHAPTER 5.
THE HOMESTRETCH—INVESTING FOR RETIREMENT IN YOUR 60s AND BEYOND

When you enter your 60s, you are entering the decade in which you are most likely to retire. At least that is what the statistics show. People have been waiting longer to retire and that trend has been going on for some time now, but the average retirement age for men is around 65 and for women it is just over 62.

Year of birth	Full retirement age (FRA)	Months between age 62 and FRA	$1,000 benefit taken at 62 is reduced to...	Percent reduction	$500 spousal benefit taken at 62 is reduced to...	Percent reduction
1937 or earlier	65	36	$ 800	20.00%	$ 375	25.00%
1938	65 and two months	38	$ 791	20.83%	$ 370	25.83%
1939	65 and four months	40	$ 783	21.67%	$ 366	26.67%
1940	65 and six months	42	$ 775	22.50%	$ 362	27.50%
1941	65 and eight months	44	$ 766	23.33%	$ 358	28.33%
1942	65 and 10 months	46	$ 758	24.17%	$ 354	29.17%
1943-1954	66	48	$ 750	25.00%	$ 350	30.00%
1955	66 and two months	50	$ 741	25.83%	$ 345	30.83%
1956	66 and four months	52	$ 733	26.67%	$ 341	31.67%
1957	66 and six months	54	$ 725	27.50%	$ 337	32.50%
1958	66 and eight months	56	$ 716	28.33%	$ 333	33.33%
1959	66 and ten months	58	$ 708	29.17%	$ 329	34.17%
1960 and later	67	60	$ 700	30.00%	$ 325	35.00%

The minimum age for full benefits from Social Security has been gradually increasing, too, and that might be having an impact on when people retire. If you aren't familiar with how the age has been changed, the table on page 63 will help.

The fact is that your 60s will likely be separated into two periods: post-retirement and pre-retirement. You will likely work through at least a few years of the decade and then shift away from working to retirement. You will be living off of a combination of a pension if you have one, Social Security and then the investment income your retirement funds produce. And that is the order in which you should count on them.

If you have a pension, hopefully it is your primary source of retirement income. Social Security would be a secondary source and distributions from your retirement accounts should make up for any shortcomings.

This brings us to your investment accounts and how they should be allocated and the purposes they will serve. Hopefully you have retirement accounts as well as a regular investment account. At this point, you will want to put the most importance on protecting your assets and growth is far less important. Less than 40% of your investments should be in stocks at this point and even those limited stock investments should be in the safest of funds.

If the market is oversold and the pessimism is high, you can treat it as a special circumstance and perhaps get a little more aggressive with your investment selections. If the market is overbought and the sentiment shows excessive optimism, at this point you might not want more than 10% to 20% of your portfolio in stock funds. Any stock investments should be inside the retirement accounts, or at least the vast majority should be held there to minimize current tax obligations.

Outside your retirement account, you should start building investments that produce income. In the pre-retirement stage, you can start building a portfolio of individual municipal bonds or "muni" bond funds to produce as much tax-free income as possible. While they have been discussed before, let's look at muni bonds and how they are or aren't taxed.

Muni bonds are not subject to federal income tax. If the issuer is in the state you live in, you can also avoid state income tax and possibly even local income tax if your area has one and the issuer is a local one. Because you are still working, you want to minimize the amount of income being produced from your investments as much as possible. This is why you keep the higher growth investments inside retirement accounts as much as possible.

If you can start setting up tax-free, income-producing investments prior to retirement, it will have the least impact on your current tax situation. There aren't always an abundance of quality bonds available, so you don't want to wait until the day you retire to start buying them. If you start a few years before retirement, you can build a higher-quality portfolio of bonds.

TAX IMPACT

You are on the cusp of retirement and have likely peaked in your earned income. Now is the time to start getting tax-free income flowing in your direction. This will reduce or maintain your current tax status and your retirement accounts are still growing tax-free. You can also look at dividend-paying stocks to generate income, but if the stocks start climbing and you end up selling them at a profit, it becomes a taxable capital gain. Be careful.

TRADITIONAL IRA, 401(K) AND ROTH IRA

One form of a retirement account that hasn't been brought up yet is the Roth IRA. The Roth is different in that your contributions are made with dollars upon which you have already paid income taxes. Because these are post-tax contributions, the distributions later aren't taxed and the capital gains made while the assets are in the account aren't taxed, either. There are limitations to the Roth in terms of who can open one and the account has to be open for five years before the distributions are made.

As of 2018, the maximum income levels for contribution to a Roth are $135,000 for single filers and $199,000 for married couples who file jointly. Just like with traditional IRAs, the maximum contribution is $5,500 if you are under 50 and $6,500 if you are 50 or older.

One of the biggest differences between a Roth IRA and a traditional IRA is how distributions are handled. It is worth repeating that withdrawals from a Roth aren't taxed as long as they have been in the account for more than five years. But the really big difference is that you don't have to start taking distributions from a Roth at any point. With the traditional IRA, you have to start taking distributions in the year you reach 70 and a half. It doesn't matter whether you need the money or not, you must start taking distributions. Having to take distributions could have a huge impact on your taxable income.

Both IRA types allow owners to start taking distributions at age 59 and a half without a penalty. The only difference here is that the money being withdrawn from a Roth IRA had to have been in the account at least five years in order to avoid a penalty.

Because there is never a required distribution from the Roth, they have become popular wealth transfer vehicles. If you are retired and don't really need the money, you can pass it on to your heirs and they won't face withdrawal penalties or taxes. They may have to pay estate taxes, but not income taxes on any withdrawals from a Roth.

One popular strategy is to convert traditional IRAs or 401(k) assets to a Roth IRA. This is tricky because you will have to pay taxes on the distribution amount from the traditional IRA or 401(k), but it will grow tax-free and then you don't have to take mandatory distributions.

One way this can be handled to minimize the tax consequences is to plan the conversion for a year when you know your income will be lower, or perhaps stretch small conversions over several years. For instance, if you plan to retire when you are 65 and expect to retire in the first quarter of the year, your total income for that year will be much lower than it would have been if you worked the whole year. This would be an ideal year to convert assets to a Roth IRA. You just want to be careful with the amount so that you don't bump yourself up to a higher tax bracket with the conversion amount.

TAX IMPACT

Up to this point, your focus has been on keeping your current tax status as low as possible. Now you are looking at keeping your taxes as low as possible in the future. This is where Roth conversions come in to play. It is also where municipal bonds come in, as well as dividend-paying domestic stocks. You are building income streams with the least amount of impact on taxable income.

REAL DAILY

WHEN TO START DRAWING FROM SOCIAL SECURITY

Believe it or not, there are instances where you should start to draw on your Social Security benefits before the full retirement age. If you have been successful in building your retirement accounts and will have plenty of income streams, you may be better off starting to receive Social Security payments earlier. That's because Social Security benefits above $25,000 are subject to taxes for single-filers and anything above $32,000 for married couples filing a joint return.

If you don't have enough set aside for retirement, obviously you would be better off waiting in order to draw as much as possible from Social Security and pay the taxes then. However, if you have enough investment income and other sources of income that you don't really need the maximum payment from Social Security, you may be able to lower your taxes by starting to take the benefits when you turn 62. That is the minimum age to start receiving Social Security payments.

This can be a tricky situation. You don't want to make the mistake of taking Social Security early and then end up not having enough income years later. Many of these scenarios should be discussed with a tax professional—such as Roth IRA conversion options and when to start drawing Social Security. Everything requires planning. Even if you plan perfectly, however, tax laws can change.

TAX IMPACT

Avoiding paying taxes in retirement is the goal here, but it is better to pay a little bit in taxes than not have enough income to live on. If you decide to start receiving Social Security benefits early, you want to make certain that you will have enough alternate income streams to meet any obligations that you have.

CAPITAL LOSSES AND HOW YOU CAN BENEFIT FROM THEM

Up until now the focus has been on avoiding paying taxes on our capital gains and keeping as much of your investments in retirement accounts where the investments grow tax-free. However, there are benefits that can be had from capital losses in a taxable account. If you sell an investment at a loss, it can be used to cancel out capital gains.

The end result is no new taxes are levied. If your losses are greater than the gains, you can use up to $3,000 of losses per year to reduce your income. If the loss is greater than $3,000, the remaining loss can be carried forward to the next year to offset capital gains or to reduce income.

Once again, you want to focus on the long run and not just sell an investment because it is at a loss. You also shouldn't hang on to an investment that has jumped sharply just so you don't have to pay taxes on the gains. It is better to pay taxes on a gain than to not have any gains at all. Of course, you can manage when you take capital gains in order to minimize the tax consequences.

Let's say you have an investment that you have owned for 11 months and it has jumped sharply in price. Perhaps you are worried that it has gone up too much and that it will start to fall. If you sell it now, you create a short-term capital gain and that gain will be taxed at your ordinary income tax rate. If you hold the investment for another month, however, you have held it for more than a year and it becomes a long-term capital gain and subject to a maximum tax rate of 20%.

You could weigh the options and see how much the taxes will differ, then compare that to how much you think you would lose if the investment drops sharply, and how soon.

FILING STATUS AND ANNUAL INCOME - 2018					LONG-TERM CAPITAL GAIN RATE
SINGLE	MARRIED FILING JOINTLY OR QUALIFIED WIDOW(ER)	MARRIED FILING SEPARATELY	HEAD OF HOUSEHOLD	TRUSTS AND ESTATES	
$0-$38,600	$0-$77,200	$0-$38,600	$0-$51,700	$0-$2,600	0%
$38,601-$425,800	$77,201-$479,000	$38,601-$239,500	$51,701-$452,400	$2,601-$12,700	15%
Over $425,800	Over $479,000	Over $239,500	Over $452,400	Over $12,700	20%

MAXIMIZING YOUR RETIREMENT INCOME

The entirety of this book is focused on maximizing your retirement accounts and income while minimizing taxes all along the way. The bulk of the material in the earlier chapters was focused on growing and protecting your investments, both inside your retirement accounts and outside of them. Now that you are in your 60s, there are three main priorities: Protecting your assets against losses, making sure you have enough income coming in, and minimizing your taxes in retirement.

These themes won't really change much once you retire. The income needed to enjoy retirement is likely going to be similar whether you are 68 or 75, so that part won't change drastically. By minimizing the taxes you pay in retirement, you maximize the income you get to keep.

TAX IMPACT

The last thing you want in retirement is to get stuck with a big tax bill while you are on a fixed income. Planning any changes for appropriate times can help reduce any tax consequences. Using appropriate investment vehicles, like municipal bonds, can produce tax-free income. Pay attention to how long investments are held to make sure capital gains are treated as long-term gains whenever possible. All of these things can reduce your taxable income in your retirement years.

CHAPTER 6.
OPPORTUNITIES AND THREATS FOR YOUR RETIREMENT

Throughout the sections on the different cycles of your investment portfolio, the terms "special circumstances" or "under normal conditions" are used quite often. The idea is that you need to make adjustments to your allocations when the market is in extreme situations.

The most common situations that were mentioned were when the market is overbought or oversold and when the sentiment toward the market is too optimistic or too pessimistic. In order to determine where the market is and when to make changes, you need to understand the tools that can tell you these things. Let's take a look at some of those tools.

OVERBOUGHT/OVERSOLD INDICATORS

There are probably 100 indicators that try to determine whether a stock or index is overbought or oversold. Sometimes, you will hear them called "oscillators." These indicators all have their fans for different reasons and they all have their detractors as well. One of the easier ones to understand is the Relative Strength Index (RSI) and it happens to be one of the more popular ones.

Without getting too technical, the RSI measures the recent gains and losses to gauge the speed and amount of change in a stock or index. The traditional key levels are 70 and 30, with 70 marking an overbought reading and 30 marking an oversold reading. You don't need to know the math to know how to use it.

Traders use the 10-day RSI as a short-term indicator, but that isn't what you want to do. You are looking at the long-term and that's why you want to use a long-term indicator. The math for the RSI works the same whether it is the 10-day or 10-month. For making allocation changes to your retirement account, the 10-month RSI is a far more appropriate indicator.

The chart on Page 74 is the monthly chart on the SPDR S&P 500 ETF (SPY). You can see the 10-month RSI below the price chart. In this case, the levels that are marked with red lines are the 80 level and the 30 level.

RELATIVE STRENGTH INDEX

Percent Bullish

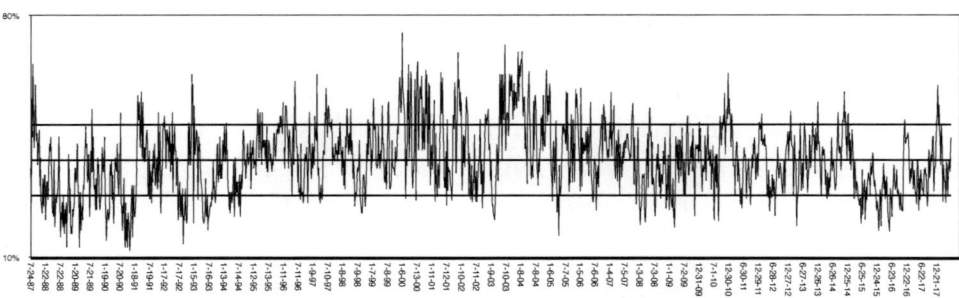

On the bottom of this chart, you can see how the 10-month RSI hit the 80 level in late 2006 and remained above it for a good part of 2007. It then dips all the way down below 20 in late 2008. It moves back up to the 80 level again in 2013 and flirts with it for the better part of two years. It moved up above the mark again in early 2017 and then moved all the way up above 90 before the market hit a rough patch in early 2018.

It isn't a perfect indicator and that is why you wouldn't want to jump out of stocks completely when the 80 level is hit, but lowering your equity allocation in 2007 would have protected more of your portfolio from the huge selloff. Likewise, when the RSI hit 30 in 2002 and 2008, you would have been allocating more assets to equities and that would have boosted your returns.

Keep in mind that your goal shouldn't be to time the market perfectly at the exact high or exact low. Your goal should be to protect your assets against a major bear market like the ones we saw in 2000-2002 and 2007-2009.

Use your indicators to raise and lower stock allocations with the goal of protecting against major downturns or to take advantage of major lows. You don't want to jump from a 70% stock allocation to 10% just because the 10-month RSI is at 80. Perhaps you lower the allocation to 60% because the RSI is at 80. Then you lower it another 10% if it hits 85 and then lower it again if the 10-month moving average crosses below the 20-month.

TAX IMPACT

Using a step-by-step process, such as the one above, to lower your stock holdings would have helped your portfolio tremendously during the two bear markets.

Most allocation changes will be made inside retirement accounts, or at least they should be. Because they are made in the retirement accounts, there isn't much of a tax impact prior to retirement. Where these allocation changes help you the most is in the amount you have to invest once you do retire. Allocation changes should be made with the long-term in mind, any taxes generated should be of secondary concern to protecting your assets.

SENTIMENT INDICATORS AND HOW TO READ THEM

The other factor that was mentioned as something to watch in order to make allocation changes was the sentiment toward the market. These indicators aren't as abundant as the overbought/oversold indicators, but they are every bit as useful.

Some sentiment indicators are easy to locate while others are a little more difficult to find. One of the easiest ones to find is the Conference Board's Consumer Confidence Index. While it isn't a direct sentiment indicator for the market, there is certainly a correlation in the movement between the two. When the market is rising, consumer confidence tends to rise concurrently. When consumer confidence gets too high and then starts falling, the market and the U.S. economy tend to lose steam as well.

If you look at the chart, you can see how the S&P 500 and consumer confidence top, trend and bottom at the same time. Consumer confidence was high and stayed elevated in the late 90s, but when it started falling in late 2000, it was a sign of things to come. When it hit bottom in late 2002, it was a sign of better things on the way. The same pattern repeats in 2007 and 2009.

You can find the consumer confidence report on the Conference Board's website and on the economic calendars from Yahoo Finance, Briefing.com, the Wall Street Journal and so forth.

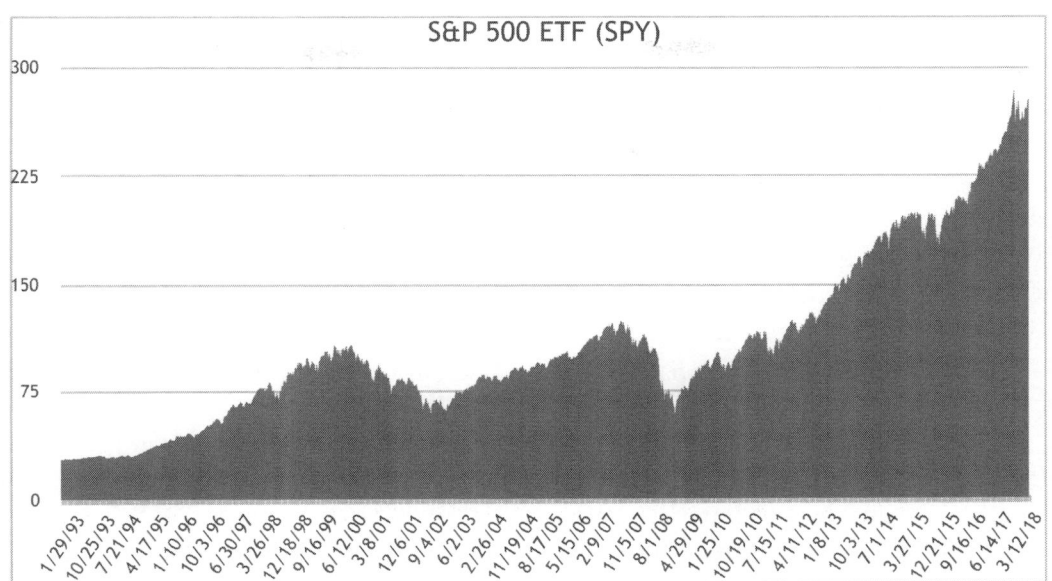

S&P 500 ETF (SPY)

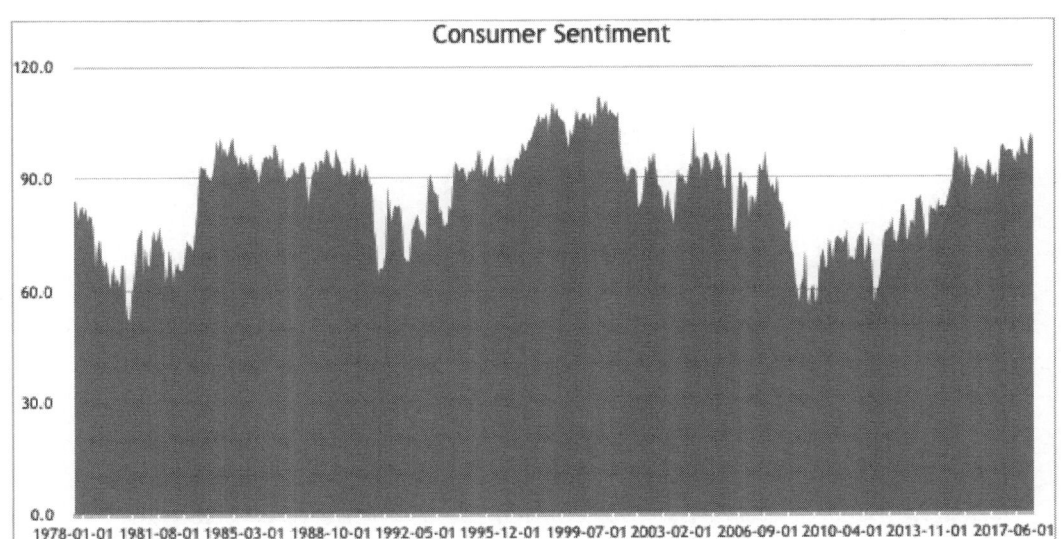

Consumer Sentiment

Another well-known sentiment indicator is the Investors Intelligence Sentiment Survey. This one is a little harder to find as it is subscription based and the fee is pretty high for an individual investor. You can usually find the most recent numbers by simply typing "recent Investors Intelligence survey" into your search engine.

Like the Consumer Confidence survey, you want to view the Investors Intelligence report from a contrarian viewpoint. When the ratio of bulls to bears is too high, that is usually a warning that the market is overly loved and you should consider scaling back your equity allocation.

Like the RSI, it isn't a perfect signal, but it can help you avoid big losses. You see on the chart below how the ratio was over 3:1 in late 2007 before the bear market and it was above 5:1 in January 2018 before the decline started then. It is too early to tell if that was a long-term peak in the market or if it is just a minor correction.

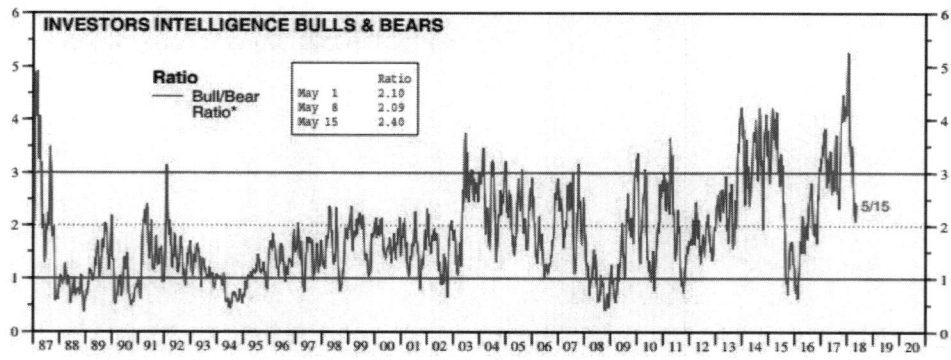

Quite simply, the reason a stock or the market goes up is because there are more buyers than sellers. The reason a stock or the market goes down is because there are more sellers than buyers. Market sentiment can help investors tell when the chance of having more buyers than sellers is most likely and vice versa.

COVERED-CALL WRITING STRATEGY

One strategy that you may hear about that can help generate income in retirement, particularly if you own a lot of stock, is a covered-call writing strategy. Here's how it works: You buy or own the underlying stock and then you write call options where the strike is higher than the current price. You collect a premium for selling the call, that is, the right for someone else to buy your shares under certain circumstances. If the stock doesn't move above the specific strike, the option expires worthless and the premium is your gain.

Let's try a specific example with a familiar company. At time of writing, IBM is trading at $143.30. The June 18 $150-strike call is priced at $0.25. Options represent 100 shares, so the $0.25 is actually worth $25 because it is multiplied times 100. For these options to be exercised by the expiration date, the stock would have to rise by 4.7% over three weeks.

If you own 1,000 shares of IBM and want to write covered-calls against those shares, you could write as many as 10 calls for $25 each and that would generate $250 of income for you. You could repeat this process month after month. But there are several things you have to keep in mind when using a covered-call strategy.

First, covered-calls that work like you hope and expire worthless are treated as income and are taxable at your income tax rate. If the stock is called away, you are taxed on the capital gains, long or short depending on how long you owned the shares.

Secondly, if you own 1,000 shares and write 10 calls, you risk getting all 1,000 shares called away from you. That is what it is called when the options close above the strike price on expiration day and the options are exercised. It means that your shares are taken away from you at a price of $150 per share—the strike price. If you don't want all of the shares at risk (say you want to keep dividend income coming in, or you just like the stock), you would not want to write 10 calls. Instead, perhaps put only half of the shares at risk of being called away and write five calls.

This strategy should be used carefully as you don't want to generate a huge long-term capital gain. By writing covered-calls on a stock you have owned for a long time, you could end up creating a big tax bill for yourself.

For instance, you may own shares of your employer that have been purchased at a discount over the years or have been given to you as a perk or bonus. Writing covered-calls against these shares is an ideal way to generate income, but you don't want the options to get exercised and have your shares called away at a higher price than you paid. That would generate a long-term capital gain and potentially bump your taxes up considerably. Nevertheless, writing covered-calls can be a legitimate and powerful way to create income with relatively little risk.

TAX IMPACT

A covered-call strategy is a great way to generate income, but you have to be aware that the gains generated are taxable. If some or all of the shares you own get called away, it could generate a capital gain. Whether it is a long-term or short-term capital gain will depend on how long you have owned the shares. You will owe taxes on the income, if any, as well.

USING BOND LADDERS TO PROTECT AGAINST CHANGING RATES

One of the greatest risks to fixed-income investments is a big change in interest rates. If you buy a bond today and interest rates rise over the next year, the bond you bought today is going to be less valuable because the price of the bond, its market value, will go down in order to bring the yield up to match current rates. If you have to sell the bond for one reason or another, you could end up taking a loss on the bond because the price is down.

Think of a bond like a car. As your vehicle ages, you expect its value to decline. It has more miles on it and less life ahead. Newer cars come on the market and perhaps offer a better value for the investment.

As interest rates rise, that same kind of used vs. new interplay can damage the value of existing bonds. Of course, if interest rates fall, the opposite could happen. Older bonds maintain their value simply because they pay higher rates than new bonds. Everyone loves a reliable old Honda and they seem to keep their value forever. In a bond bull market, like the one we've seen for the past three decades, all bonds seemed to be Hondas. That's changing.

When bond prices go up, yield goes down. When price goes down, yield goes up. If you are relying on the income generated from bonds for your retirement income, changing interest rates can have a huge impact on both the value of your portfolio and the income it generates.

One way to protect yourself from big changes in rates is to build what is called a bond ladder. Building a bond ladder requires you to purchase individual bonds that have staggered maturity dates. For instance, you could buy bonds that mature every year for the next 10 years. If interest rates go up over the coming years, the maturing bonds can be replaced with bonds that generate more income for you. Conversely, if interest rates fall, the bonds that mature will be replaced with ones paying less interest, but you will still have other bonds that pay more, softening the impact.

Bond ladders can be used with any form of bond—government, municipal, corporate bonds. They can also be used as a strategic way to meet annual income needs. You could buy bonds that mature every year for the next 30 years, typically the longest maturities issued.

If you know you need an additional $10,000 in income each year, buying bonds that mature each year means you can use the bonds to generate income and then, when they mature, you use the principal amount for added income or to replace maturing bonds.

Another possible use for a bond ladder would be to meet a specific expense at a specific time. If you know you are going to have large expenses coming due at specific dates, you can stagger your bond ladder such that you have bonds maturing just before the expenses are due.

TAX IMPACT

Depending upon the types of bonds you use in a bond ladder, some or all of the income generated from interest payments could be taxable. Of course, if you use municipal bonds you can greatly reduce the tax impact of the interest payments. Using a bond ladder can be tricky and may require the assistance of a professional investment advisor.

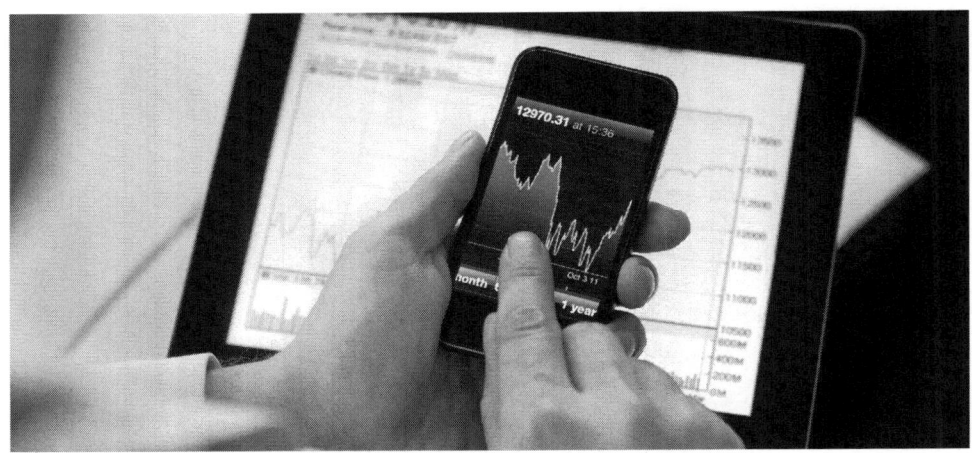

CHAPTER 7.
LIVE ON MORE DURING RETIREMENT

Up to this point, the focus has been entirely on your investments, inside and outside of retirement accounts—how to use different investment vehicles, how to change your allocations, how to structure your investments, and so on. But there are changes you can make in retirement that will help you generate income and avoid paying taxes if at all possible.

If you have reached retirement and discovered that you don't have enough income to cover your living expenses via Social Security and other resources, there are moves you can make to add to your income or possibly make your income go farther.

MOVE TO A STATE WITH NO INCOME TAX

Many retirees may be hesitant to move away from their home area where they have children, close friends or other family nearby, but it might be necessary in order to stretch your retirement income. Various states have a wide range of tax rates, ranging from zero to as high as 13.3% in California.

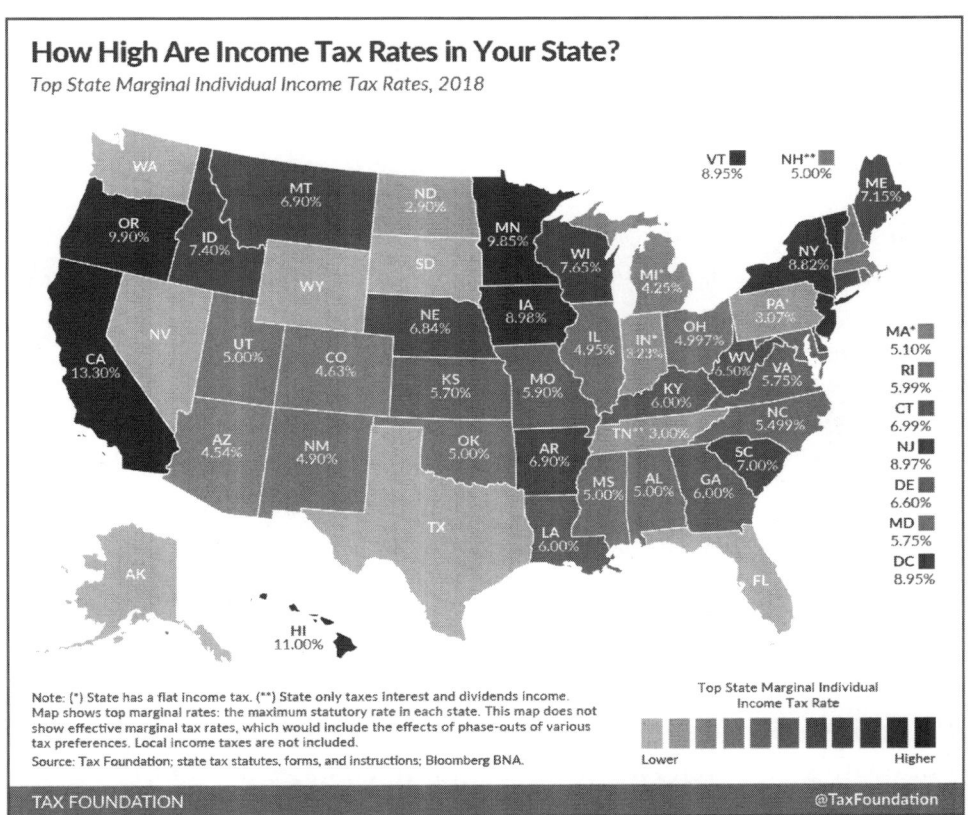

Having a state income tax cut into your income can be substantial. For instance, the maximum tax rate in Georgia is 6% and that rate kicks in at only $10,000 of adjusted gross income.

A retired Georgia resident that has $100,000 of income that is completely taxable, thus, would pay $6,000 in state income tax. Meanwhile the state just to the south, Florida, has no state income tax. Consider that moving across a state line amounts to a $500 monthly difference in income. Now you know one of the reasons so many retirees move to Florida.

In all, there are seven states with no state income tax: Alaska, Florida, Nevada, South Dakota, Texas, Washington and Wyoming. Given the moderate temperatures in the winter in Texas and Florida, the two states have been preferred destinations for retirees for years.

But it's not all about income. While some states don't have income taxes, they might have higher sales tax and real estate tax rates to offset the lack of income tax revenue. For instance, real estate taxes in Texas are among the highest in the country.

New Jersey has the highest real estate taxes in the country and they have one of the highest income tax rates as well. Hawaii on the other hand has one of the highest income tax rates with a maximum rate of 11%, but it ranks last in terms of its real estate tax rate. (See Appendix A)

When it comes to paying sales tax, Louisiana ranks as the highest with an estimated combined local and state rate of 10.02%. Tennessee ranks second in this category with a combined rate of 9.46%. Arkansas (9.41%), Washington (9.18%) and Alabama (9.1%) are the only other states with a rate over 9%. There are also three states that don't have a sales tax—Delaware, Montana and Oregon. (See Appendix B)

TAX IMPACT

If you are trying to stretch your retirement income and you are considering a move to another state, you will want to evaluate all three of these taxes—income, real estate and sales taxes. A lower income tax rate or no income tax may be offset by the real estate tax you pay or the sales tax you pay. If you plan on renting, you won't have to pay real estate taxes directly, but it will more than likely be made up for with a higher rental rate. If you are an above-average consumer who shops more than the average retiree, a higher sales tax could have an adverse effect.

REVERSE MORTGAGES

One potential source of income in retirement that you have probably heard advertised but may not know that much about is a reverse mortgage. With a reverse mortgage, instead of borrowing a big chunk of money to buy your house, you are getting money to spend on whatever you want from the house you already own.

There are different ways of structuring a reverse mortgage. You can borrow a lump sum for medical expenses or renovations, for instance. You also can receive monthly payments from the mortgage company, if you so choose, as a supplement to your Social Security income.

As with any mortgage, there are limitations on how much you can borrow. With reverse mortgages there are additional requirements as well. For instance, you must be at least 62 years of age to qualify for a reverse mortgage. The amount you can borrow is restricted based on the age of the youngest borrower.

So if a couple wants to use a reverse mortgage to supplement their monthly income, the amount they can borrow will be determined based on the age of the younger spouse.

Of course, there are other factors as well. The value of the home and the credit history of the borrowers are two examples. You should also keep in mind that a reverse mortgage is only available on your primary residence. Should you move out of the home, the mortgage must be paid in full. That includes if you move in to an assisted living facility.

The good news is that reverse mortgage payments are considered loan advances and therefore they aren't taxed as income. They usually don't affect your Social Security or Medicaid benefits either.

Those are the pros of doing a reverse mortgage, and of course there are cons as well. The fees and interest rates for reverse mortgages tend to be higher than they are with traditional mortgages. Many reverse mortgages can't be refinanced, so the terms should be considered carefully before an agreement is signed.

One concern that seems to be common on reverse mortgages is how and when it gets paid off. As was mentioned before, if you move out of the house for any reason, the mortgage must be paid off. If a couple uses a reverse mortgage and one spouse passes away, the other borrower doesn't have to pay off the loan—if he or she remains in the home.

Some borrowers are concerned that reverse mortgages could put a burden on their heirs. One thing to remember about reverse mortgages, though, is they are non-recourse loans. This means that if the home sells for less than the loan amount, your heirs can't be forced to pay the balance. Only the home can to be used to repay the loan; the lender can't go after any other assets.

TAX IMPACT

Reverse mortgages aren't for everyone and they should be given careful consideration before any documents are signed. That being said, if your retirement income isn't providing you enough money to live on and you qualify for a reverse mortgage, they can be a great source of non-taxable revenue.

DOWNSIZING YOUR HOME

One last thing that retirees can use to build assets is their home. If you don't need the space that you once did and don't mind moving from your long-time home, capital gains on the sale of your home have some special exemptions. If you have lived in your home for at least two of the past five years, you may qualify for the home-sale capital gain exemption. This exemption is up to $250,000 for individuals and $500,000 for joint filers.

What this means is that you can potentially sell your house for $500,000 more than you paid for it and pay not a penny in federal taxes. If you and your spouse bought your house for $100,000 and it has appreciated to the point that you can sell it for $600,000, you can sell it and not have to pay taxes on the gains.

Having $500,000 to invest can go a long way toward building an income-producing portfolio. Of course, you will either have to buy another home to live in or rent one. But consider that you could take part of the gain to buy a condo or townhouse and still have money left over.

If you invest $500,000 in a portfolio of income-producing mutual funds that yields 3.6%, that's $18,000 a year in income. Of course, you will have to take your tax scenario in to account.

TAX IMPACT

Having a possible $500,000 tax exemption has to be taken into consideration, even if you have sufficient retirement income. Of course very few people are going to have that much of a capital gain in their home. If you do have a considerable capital gain on your home, you may want to consider selling it and moving the assets into investments. This could save your heirs a considerable tax burden after you pass away.

APPENDIX A. REAL ESTATE PROPERTY TAXES BY STATE (SOURCE: WALLETHUB)

RANK (1=LOWEST)	STATE	EFFECTIVE REAL-ESTATE TAX RATE	ANNUAL TAXES ON $185K HOME*	STATE MEDIAN HOME VALUE	ANNUAL TAXES ON HOME PRICED AT STATE MEDIAN VALUE
1	HAWAII	0.27%	$501	$538,400	$1,459
2	ALABAMA	0.43%	$791	$128,500	$550
3	LOUISIANA	0.51%	$934	$148,300	$750
4	DELAWARE	0.55%	$1,009	$233,100	$1,274
5	D.C.	0.56%	$1,026	$506,100	$2,811
6	COLORADO	0.57%	$1,058	$264,600	$1,516
6	SOUTH CAROLINA	0.57%	$1,056	$143,600	$821
8	WEST VIRGINIA	0.59%	$1,082	$107,400	$629
9	WYOMING	0.61%	$1,130	$199,900	$1,223
10	ARKANSAS	0.63%	$1,161	$114,700	$721
11	UTAH	0.67%	$1,240	$224,600	$1,508
12	TENNESSEE	0.75%	$1,376	$146,000	$1,088
13	IDAHO	0.76%	$1,404	$167,900	$1,276
13	NEW MEXICO	0.76%	$1,408	$161,600	$1,232
15	ARIZONA	0.77%	$1,427	$176,900	$1,367
15	NEVADA	0.77%	$1,425	$191,600	$1,478
17	CALIFORNIA	0.79%	$1,461	$409,300	$3,237
17	VIRGINIA	0.79%	$1,467	$248,400	$1,973
19	MISSISSIPPI	0.80%	$1,470	$105,700	$841
20	KENTUCKY	0.85%	$1,579	$126,100	$1,078
20	MONTANA	0.85%	$1,570	$199,700	$1,698
22	NORTH CAROLINA	0.86%	$1,581	$157,100	$1,345
23	INDIANA	0.87%	$1,606	$126,500	$1,100
24	OKLAHOMA	0.89%	$1,638	$121,300	$1,076
25	GEORGIA	0.93%	$1,712	$152,400	$1,413
26	MISSOURI	1.00%	$1,842	$141,200	$1,408
27	FLORIDA	1.02%	$1,885	$166,800	$1,702
28	NORTH DAKOTA	1.05%	$1,947	$164,000	$1,729
29	WASHINGTON	1.06%	$1,962	$269,300	$2,860
30	OREGON	1.07%	$1,970	$247,200	$2,637

APPENDIX A. REAL ESTATE PROPERTY TAXES BY STATE (SOURCE: WALLETHUB)

RANK (1=LOWEST)	STATE	EFFECTIVE REAL-ESTATE TAX RATE	ANNUAL TAXES ON $185K HOME*	STATE MEDIAN HOME VALUE	ANNUAL TAXES ON HOME PRICED AT STATE MEDIAN VALUE
31	MARYLAND	1.10%	$2,030	$290,400	$3,191
32	MINNESOTA	1.17%	$2,155	$191,500	$2,234
33	ALASKA	1.19%	$2,190	$257,100	$3,048
34	MASSACHUSETTS	1.21%	$2,238	$341,000	$4,132
35	MAINE	1.32%	$2,444	$176,000	$2,329
35	SOUTH DAKOTA	1.32%	$2,446	$146,700	$1,943
37	KANSAS	1.40%	$2,580	$135,300	$1,890
38	IOWA	1.50%	$2,762	$132,800	$1,986
39	PENNSYLVANIA	1.55%	$2,867	$167,700	$2,603
40	OHIO	1.56%	$2,890	$131,900	$2,064
41	NEW YORK	1.65%	$3,057	$286,300	$4,738
41	RHODE ISLAND	1.65%	$3,047	$238,200	$3,929
43	MICHIGAN	1.71%	$3,158	$127,800	$2,185
44	VERMONT	1.78%	$3,285	$218,900	$3,893
45	NEBRASKA	1.83%	$3,371	$137,300	$2,506
46	TEXAS	1.86%	$3,435	$142,700	$2,654
47	WISCONSIN	1.95%	$3,602	$167,000	$3,257
48	CONNECTICUT	2.02%	$3,733	$269,300	$5,443
49	NEW HAMPSHIRE	2.19%	$4,038	$239,700	$5,241
50	ILLINOIS	2.32%	$4,288	$174,800	$4,058
51	NEW JERSEY	2.40%	$4,437	$316,400	$7,601

*$184,700 IS THE MEDIAN HOME VALUE IN THE U.S. AS OF 2016, THE YEAR OF THE MOST RECENT AVAILABLE DATA.

APPENDIX B. SALES TAXES BY STATE
(SOURCE: TAX FOUNDATION)

STATE	STATE TAX RATE	RANK	AVG. LOCAL TAX RATE (A)	COMBINED RATE	COMBINED RANK	MAX LOCAL TAX RATE
ALABAMA	4.00%	40	5.10%	9.10%	5	7.50%
ALASKA	0.00%	46	1.76%	1.76%	46	7.50%
ARIZONA	5.60%	28	2.73%	8.33%	11	5.30%
ARKANSAS	6.50%	9	2.91%	9.41%	3	5.125%
CALIFORNIA (B)	7.25%	1	1.29%	8.54%	9	2.50%
COLORADO	2.90%	45	4.62%	7.52%	16	8.30%
CONNECTICUT	6.35%	12	0.00%	6.35%	33	0.00%
DELAWARE	0.00%	46	0.00%	0.00%	47	0.00%
FLORIDA	6.00%	16	0.80%	6.80%	28	2.00%
GEORGIA	4.00%	40	3.15%	7.15%	20	4.90%
HAWAII (C)	4.00%	40	0.35%	4.35%	45	0.50%
IDAHO	6.00%	16	0.03%	6.03%	37	3.00%
ILLINOIS	6.25%	13	2.45%	8.70%	7	4.75%
INDIANA	7.00%	2	0.00%	7.00%	22	0.00%
IOWA	6.00%	16	0.80%	6.80%	27	1.00%
KANSAS	6.50%	9	2.18%	8.68%	8	4.00%
KENTUCKY	6.00%	16	0.00%	6.00%	38	0.00%
LOUISIANA	5.00%	33	5.02%	10.02%	1	7.00%
MAINE	5.50%	29	0.00%	5.50%	42	0.00%
MARYLAND	6.00%	16	0.00%	6.00%	38	0.00%
MASSACHUSETTS	6.25%	13	0.00%	6.25%	35	0.00%
MICHIGAN	6.00%	16	0.00%	6.00%	38	0.00%
MINNESOTA	6.875%	6	0.55%	7.42%	17	2.00%
MISSISSIPPI	7.00%	2	0.07%	7.07%	21	1.00%
MISSOURI	4.225%	39	3.80%	8.03%	14	5.39%
MONTANA (D)	0.00%	46	0.00%	0.00%	47	0.00%
NEBRASKA	5.50%	29	1.39%	6.89%	25	2.00%
NEVADA	6.85%	7	1.29%	8.14%	13	1.42%
NEW HAMPSHIRE	0.00%	46	0.00%	0.00%	47	0.00%
NEW JERSEY (E)	6.625%	8	-0.03%	6.60%	30	3.31%

APPENDIX B. SALES TAXES BY STATE
(SOURCE: TAX FOUNDATION)

STATE	STATE TAX RATE	RANK	AVG. LOCAL TAX RATE (A)	COMBINED RATE	COMBINED RANK	MAX LOCAL TAX RATE
NEW MEXICO (C)	5.125%	32	2.54%	7.66%	15	4.1250%
NEW YORK	4.00%	40	4.49%	8.49%	10	4.875%
NORTH CAROLINA	4.75%	36	2.20%	6.95%	24	2.75%
NORTH DAKOTA	5.00%	33	1.80%	6.80%	26	3.50%
OHIO	5.75%	27	1.40%	7.15%	19	2.25%
OKLAHOMA	4.50%	37	4.41%	8.91%	6	6.50%
OREGON	0.00%	46	0.00%	0.00%	47	0.00%
PENNSYLVANIA	6.00%	16	0.34%	6.34%	34	2.00%
RHODE ISLAND	7.00%	2	0.00%	7.00%	22	0.00%
SOUTH CAROLINA	6.00%	16	1.37%	7.37%	18	3.00%
SOUTH DAKOTA (C)	4.50%	37	1.90%	6.40%	31	4.50%
TENNESSEE	7.00%	2	2.46%	9.46%	2	2.75%
TEXAS	6.25%	13	1.92%	8.17%	12	2.00%
UTAH (B)	5.95%	26	0.82%	6.77%	29	2.65%
VERMONT	6.00%	16	0.18%	6.18%	36	1.00%
VIRGINIA (B)	5.30%	31	0.33%	5.63%	41	0.70%
WASHINGTON	6.50%	9	2.68%	9.18%	4	3.90%
WEST VIRGINIA	6.00%	16	0.37%	6.37%	32	1.00%
WISCONSIN	5.00%	33	0.42%	5.42%	44	1.75%
WYOMING	4.00%	40	1.46%	5.46%	43	2.00%
D.C.	5.75%	(27)	0.00%	5.75%	35	0.00%

STATE AND LOCAL SALES TAX RATES AS OF JANUARY 1, 2018

(a) City, county and municipal rates vary. These rates are weighted by population to compute an average local tax rate.

(b) Three states levy mandatory, statewide, local add-on sales taxes at the state level: California (1.25%), Utah (1.25%), Virginia (1%), we include these in their state sales tax.

(c) The sales taxes in Hawaii, New Mexico, North Dakota and South Dakota have broad bases that include many services.

(d) Special taxes in local resort areas are not counted here.

(e) Salem County is not subject to the statewide sales tax rate and collects a local rate of 3.3125%. New Jersey's average local score is represented as a negative.

Sources: Sales Tax Clearinghouse, Tax Foundation calculations, State Revenue Department websites.

Financial Disclaimer:

NEITHER REAL DAILY NOR ITS OWNERS, OFFICERS, DIRECTORS, EMPLOYEES, SUBSIDIARIES, AFFILIATES, LICENSORS, SERVICE PROVIDERS, CONTENT PROVIDERS AND AGENTS ARE FINANCIAL ADVISERS AND NOTHING CONTAINED ON THE SITE IS INTENDED TO BE OR TO BE CONSTRUED AS FINANCIAL ADVICE.

REAL DAILY IS NOT AN INVESTMENT ADVISORY SERVICE, IS NOT AN INVESTMENT ADVISER, AND DOES NOT PROVIDE PERSONALIZED FINANCIAL ADVICE OR ACT AS A FINANCIAL ADVISOR. REALDAILY.COM EXISTS FOR EDUCATIONAL PURPOSES ONLY, AND THE MATERIALS AND INFORMATION CONTAINED HEREIN ARE FOR GENERAL INFORMATIONAL PURPOSES ONLY.

THE EDUCATION AND INFORMATION PRESENTED HEREIN IS INTENDED FOR A GENERAL AUDIENCE AND DOES NOT PURPORT TO BE, NOR SHOULD IT BE CONSTRUED AS, SPECIFIC ADVICE TAILORED TO ANY INDIVIDUAL. YOU ARE ENCOURAGED TO DISCUSS ANY OPPORTUNITIES WITH YOUR ATTORNEY, ACCOUNTANT, FINANCIAL PROFESSIONAL OR OTHER ADVISOR.

The information contained in this program (including but not limited to content in any format) is based on sources and information reasonably believed to be accurate as of the time it was recorded or created. However, this material deals with topics that are constantly changing and are subject to ongoing changes related to technology and the market place as well as legal and related compliance issues. Therefore, the completeness and current accuracy of the materials cannot be guaranteed. These materials do not constitute legal, compliance, financial, tax, accounting, or related advice.

The end user of this information should therefore use the contents of this program and the materials as a general guideline and not as the ultimate source of current information and when appropriate the user should consult their own legal, accounting or other advisors.

Any case studies, examples, illustrations cannot guarantee that the user will achieve similar results. In fact, your results may vary significantly and factors such as your market, personal effort and many other circumstances may and will cause results to vary.

THE INFORMATION PROVIDED IN THIS PRODUCT IS SOLD AND PROVIDED ON AN "AS IS" BASIS. REAL DAILY DOES NOT PROMISE OR GUARANTEE ANY INCOME OR PARTICULAR RESULT FROM YOUR USE OF THE INFORMATION CONTAINED HEREIN. THOSE RESULTS ARE YOUR RESPONSIBILITY AS THE END USER OF THE PRODUCT. (SOME STATES DO NOT ALLOW LIMITED WARRANTIES, SO THIS MAY NOT APPLY TO YOU.) IN PARTICULAR, REAL DAILY SHALL NOT BE LIABLE TO USER OR ANY OTHER PARTY FOR ANY DAMAGES, OR COSTS, OF ANY CHARACTER INCLUDING BUT NOT LIMITED TO DIRECT OR INDIRECT, CONSEQUENTIAL, SPECIAL, INCIDENTAL, OR OTHER COSTS OR DAMAGES, IN EXCESS OF THE PURCHASE PRICE OF THE PRODUCT OR SERVICES. THESE LIMITATIONS MAY BE AFFECTED BY THE LAWS OF PARTICULAR STATES AND

NONE OF REAL DAILY, ITS OWNERS OFFICERS, DIRECTORS, EMPLOYEES, SUBSIDIARIES, AFFILIATES, LICENSORS, SERVICE PROVIDERS, CONTENT PROVIDERS AND AGENTS (ALL COLLECTIVELY HEREINAFTER REFERRED TO AS "REAL DAILY") ARE FINANCIAL ADVISERS AND NOTHING CONTAINED HEREIN IS INTENDED TO BE OR TO BE CONSTRUED AS FINANCIAL ADVICE.